Natural
Architecture

Natural Architecture

40 Earth Sheltered House Designs

Revised Edition

Charles G. Woods

VAN NOSTRAND REINHOLD COMPANY

NEW YORK   CINCINNATI   TORONTO   LONDON   MELBOURNE

Printed in the United States of America
Designed by Randolph-Padorr Black

Published by Van Nostrand Reinhold Company Inc.
135 West 50th Street
New York, New York 10020

Van Nostrand Reinhold Company Limited
Molly Millars Lane
Wokingham, Berkshire RG11 2PY, England

Van Nostrand Reinhold
480 La Trobe Street
Melbourne, Victoria 3000, Australia

Macmillan of Canada
Division of Gage Publishing Limited
164 Commander Boulevard
Agincourt, Ontario M1S 3C7, Canada

16 15 14 13 12 11 10 9 8 7 6 5 4 3 2 1

Library of Congress Cataloging in Publication Data

Woods, Charles G.
    Natural architecture.

    Bibliography: p.
    Includes index.
    1. Earth sheltered houses. 2. Organic architecture.
I. Title
NA7531.W66   1984   728   83-25913
ISBN 0-442-29256-2
ISBN 0-442-29257-0 (pbk.)

For my wife and friend
Julie Kathryn Gundlach

Table of Contents

Foreword

The cliche' "A man's home is his castle" is as much in vogue today as it was when the first pioneers settled in this country. Much of their measure of achievement was in the size of their home.

Early Americans took pride in the land they owned, worked, harvested and lived on. Unlike many of our resources today, the air was free from pollutants, the water fit to drink, and the soil rich in nutrients.

Family roots were planted across this country in various types of structures, many of them being earth sheltered. They were built into the landscape, with earth pulled around and onto them, to provide shelter from the rain, wind, snow and violent weather. Extreme cold and searing summer temperatures were reduced by this moderating condition.

Through several decades of growth, prosperity and plenty of cheap energy, housing in America became a multitude of various sized boxes built in a row and all on *top* of the ground.

It is ironic, perhaps, that we have once again returned to the earth to solve many of the ills that modern day living has brought with it. We now seek relief from the high cost of heating and cooling, which is rising each year. Maintenance expense and insurance premiums keep going up. We want protection from vandalism, and to get away from freeway and airport noises.

Earth shelter living can provide all this and more in today's contemporary society without giving up the convenience and creature comforts that we have become accustomed to. Today's earth sheltered residence is an alternative response to our changing needs in energy usage as well as lifestyles.

The successful revival of earth shelter construction in recent years has created a demand for aesthetically pleasing, environmentally sound, and cost effective designs. Up to this point, much of this emphasis has been lacking as concern has been mainly directed towards structural integrity in construction techniques.

Award winning designer Charles Woods, using his creative flair, has blended nature's organic designs into attractive structures that are appealing, efficient and settle gently and harmoniously into the landscape.

Ultimately, the homeowner decides what he likes, wants, and can afford. Housing units in the future will be down sized to fit reductions in population and family size. Multiple unit housing, such as apartments, condominiums, townhouses, etc., is beginning to reflect this pattern already.

Investment in a well designed earth sheltered home can be a rewarding step for those with foresight and with a desire to preserve the virtues that made this country great. It is not difficult to predict that earth shelter living will find its way into a high percentage of residential and commercial construction in the future.

William E. Baker, Publisher
Earth Shelter Living Magazine

Preface

These designs show my evolution in design for the last eight years, from free form designs to and through simple rectilinear plans and back to more complex curvilinear forms. These homes were designed with the average builder and client in mind; and although I do like all the designs, they are not all as organic as I prefer.

NATURAL ARCHITECTURE; designs, drawings and renderings, were completed in several different parts of the country; Pennsylvania, Florida, Illinois and Minnesota. By and large I do not feel the designs are redundant beyond a necessary point. I have tried to utilize all major construction techniques and most of the more prominent building materials that are currently used in this type of construction.

This work, originally scheduled as a three year exercise, has been completed in a year, thanks to William Baker, WEBCO Publishing, Inc., Publisher of Earth Shelter Living Magazine. I strongly suggest to those having an interest in earth shelter construction and the lifestyle that accompanies it, subscribing to this informative, bi-monthly magazine devoted entirely to this type of living around the world as well as in the U.S.

As for future organic designs, a second design book will be published approximately two years from now. It will have designs of ten detailed projects, in fact, a whole community, including multi-unit housing, office buildings, factories, churches, and more. Comments or criticisms on any of my designs are also welcome from professionals and laymen alike.

Charles G. Woods
Honesdale, Pennsylvania
August 23, 1982

Revised Edition

In this revised edition I have added five new designs and a complete set of working drawings. It is hoped that these changes and additions make this edition of NATURAL ARCHITECTURE a more useful book.

July, 1983

Photograph by Bruce Ankele

Acknowledgments

I heartily thank WEBCO Publishing, Inc., for their faith in my work and patient assistance in the publishing of this book. And, to Julie Gundlach for preliminary typing and editing.

I would especially like to thank Randy Padorr-Black, Jay Boyle, Joe Healy, Elizabeth Davidson, Al Sincavage, Dennis Blair, Warren Heinly, and Dave Eurton for their renderings and/or drawings. They did a great deal of work under pressure and did it so well. This is as much their book as mine!

Thanks to Architect Dennis Blair for teaching me much of what I know of architecture. By comparison I am aware of how much I have yet to learn.

Thanks to Mr. and Mrs. Tom Cashin and to Architerra, Inc., for permission to include drawings of their projects, and again, to Dennis Blair for his permission to include projects we worked on together. Also, my appreciation to Al Lees of *Popular Science,* the *Chicago Sun Times* and Malcolm Wells for permission to quote them on the cover of *NATURAL ARCHITECTURE.*

This book did not develop overnight as I have been helped and supported by many over the last ten years who had faith in me. I would like to thank those people in four various categories.

ARCHITECTURAL INSPIRATIONS
Frank Lloyd Wright, Louis Sullivan, Dennis Blair, Malcolm Wells.

PROFESSIONAL ASSISTANCE
In addition to those already mentioned, John Campbell Lahey, John Carl Heinrich, Phil Knudsen, James Epperson, Joseph Meyer, P.E., Ralph Anderson, and Architect Albert Sincavage.

RELATIVES
All of my relatives, too numerous to name, for their support and several for direct help with Natural Architecture; my grandmother Anne Polzin, my brother Bob Woods, and my wife Julie—they have all made it a truly "family affair."

FRIENDS
Bruce Evan Ankele, Lenore Ankele, J. Harley Chapman, Dr. Robert S. Jackson, Tom Provost, Kathy Healy, John Weidner, Bill McAllister, C.P.A, Emil Wagnes, Randy and Tia Padorr-Black, Jim and Nena McCloud-Walker, Rose Palgutta, et al., Roger Bert, Mike Lorenz, Herman and Barbara Gundlach, Sandy Scull, Joyce and The Printery, Sri Swami Rama and the Himalayan Institute, the folks at Royal Blueprint. Mr. and Mrs. Ziegler, Mr. and Mrs. Theodore Koerner III, Richard Van Leirsburg, Rabbi S. Twersky, and last but not least, Fred's Diner in Honesdale. If I've left anyone out, blame my memory, not my heart and soul.

Introduction

Philosophy of An Organic Architecture

Do we need a philosophy of architecture? That question is not a prelude to an intellectual game; it is the very foundation upon which the work of an architect or designer rests. Are we lacking a coherent philosophy of architecture? My answer: Just look around!

Look at our cities: 100-story towers of steel and glass, dehumanizing in scale, loom as clones of one another. Hubris characterizes their demeanor. The glass on all four sides mockingly attests to the lack of concern for energy conservation. There is defiance, not deference, towards nature.

Witness the chaos represented by our gas stations, our fast food restaurants, our shopping malls, and even our houses. We see a mix of Greek, Roman, Mediterranean, and contemporary design elements, sometimes in the same structure. There is no proportion, no sense of wholeness, no sense of relationship to nature, to neighbors, to history. We are drowning in an architectural sea of forms and details. We need a raft—a philosophy of architecture based on consistent principles.

I do not presume my own work to represent the ideal. But in this book I have tried to design buildings based on a set of principles. Using a term applied to the works of Wright and Sullivan (those great and lonely geniuses who almost single-handedly established a natural and rational American architecture), I characterize my designs as "organic" in the sense of 'living' and 'whole' with interdependent parts; for that is how I visualize a building. Architecture creates for humankind a second skin. It is revealing that the word "house" often symbolizes "body" in the Bible and other spiritual and religious writings.

Organic architecture is mystical as well as rational, humble as well as inspired. Its principles are wholeness, simplicity, and honesty. Organic architecture must take into an account an array of very human considerations. Besides cost and practicability, the key to living, holistic design is the environment — its geography, topology, history, climate, and color and materials.

Let us begin our look at organic architecture with the concept of wholeness, for as the foundation supports the structure of the building, so the concept of wholeness supports the philosophy of organic architecture.

The idea of nature as an organism, in a sense of a living body (pan-psychism), has a long history. It is evident in the writings of the pre-Socratic philosophers and Heraclitus and Parmenides. In the Middle Ages its champion was Spinoza, later, Hegel and Darwin. Today Nature as a living organism is seen in the developing philosophies of Samuel Alexander, A.N. Whitehead, Sri Aurobindo, and Teilhard de Chardin.

All of nature is one organic whole. Everything is interrelated in a dynamic way. Humanity (at least, the physical body, for those who believe in a separate and immortal soul) is a part of Nature. Although many have tried, humanity cannot be cleaved from and set in opposition to Nature.

We pollute Nature both physically and visually as if it is not in any way related to ourselves; whereas, in fact, it *is* ourselves. This havoc we wreak upon Nature has its origins in religious and metaphysical error. Unconsciously we ascribe to the dualism of Rene Descartes, whereby humanity is separated from Nature. This concept, with its corresponding hubris and ignorance of what humanity truly is or can become, manifests itself in ugliness. We pollute Nature first with the mind — with the concepts and ideas — and only later with toxic wastes and unsightly and dysfunctional buildings.

Architecture is great, just as art is great, when it proceeds from an intuition of the ordered relationships and the wholeness that exists in Nature. Architecture can both reveal the essence of humanity and critique it. It matters not whether one subscribes to the idea of Spinoza and the oriental philosophers that humanity has an essential nature or whether one sides with the Existentialists to declare that humanity has no essential nature other than what it wills or creates itself. Architecture holds a mirror to both these positions.

Some may feel that to impose a philosophy on architecture is to wander far from the path an architect must tread. I think not. The concept of Nature as a living and vital organic whole may be argued, but it cannot be denied. Wholism is revolutionizing medicine, psychiatry, ecology, and more. It will revolutionize architecture. We may view the works of Antonio Gaudi, Rodulf Steiner, Eric Mendelsohn, Le Corbusier, Mies Van der Rohe, Herman Finsterlin, and, of course, Frank Lloyd Wright and Louis Sullivan to see the evolutionary and revolutionary impetus of organic architecture. On the contemporary scene we may glimpse the future via the works of Malcom Wells, Paolo Soleri, and Roland Coates.

These architects and designers have accepted the obligation and duty of their professions — to design for the essence of what we are and can become. Architecture, as our reflection, should show us at our best.

Architecture tells us much about ourselves and about our past. What does the architecture of societies in the past represent?

Egypt: the striving for eternity. Greece: the pursuit of beauty and grace. Rome: the drive for power. The Gothic cathedrals of Europe: the yearning of finite beings for a transcedent God. It is not happenstance that Hitler and his architect looked to Rome as the model of Third Reich architecture. Gigantic in proportions, scale models of Speer's buildings were sometimes one hundred feet long. These small designs dwarfed human proportions as surely as the government they symbolized effaced human individuality.

We have had great architecture in America. Early colonials developed a beautifully simple architecture in response to their environment, but it was soon bogged down in duplication of ornamentation from the past. Early colonial architecture is superb compared to later gingerbread designs.

(It is interesting to note that in historical societies with a linear view of time, architecture tends to retain historical details from earlier periods. However, in non-historical societies, the so-called 'primitive' cultures—those with a cyclical view of time—one sees a more perennial architecture. For example, I submit that Roman architecture is not as great as Greek architecture, for the former superimposed the latter over its own innate Roman identity).

And what of America's architecture today? If we were to judge by influence alone, there are four or five unknown designers who would be called great. Representing over 90 percent of all housing built in the United States, their designs are familiar to us all. But if we were to judge those designs by the use of energy, cost or aesthetic standards, they would surely be seen as disasters.

We see diamond shapes in entry doors next to French provincial lanterns, next to colonial windows. I do not intend to criticize individual homeowners. Perhaps Americans expect too little of their architects. Nonetheless, their architects have failed them.

The post-modern movement continues this tradition of disaster, creating, for instance, buildings with Ionic columns and fluorescent lights painted pink and blue. These are the most famous architects around! One cannot deny they are brilliant and creative, but their misplaced creative energies serve only to degrade architecture to an indulgent, even silly, individuality.

Happily, there are beautiful exceptions. For instance the architecture of Frank Lloyd Wright was an attempt to create a truly American architecture, a departure from the hodgepodge of Greek and Roman stone details imposed on wood structures. Although Wright had, and continues to have, great influence on American architecture, his philosophy has never really taken root. His Usonia houses are incredibly beautiful. Wright, and Louis Sullivan before him, have much to offer. Why not design according to the principles they represent? That is what I have tried to do in this book. Building on the foundation of the wholeness that exists in Nature, I have used simplicity and honesty as my guiding principles.

Simplicity need not be dull, as the Japanese have shown. In all its periods, Japanese architecture is easily recognizable. Yet it has many variegated forms, and in addition to its basic simplicity it is honest.

What do we mean by honesty in architecture? Let us begin with what honesty is not. It is not asphalt shingles made to look like wood. It is not plastic made to look like stone, or rubber made to look like brick. Wood, brick, and stone are beautiful, but if they are too expensive to use, seek honest alternatives. A concrete slab floor may be scored with module lines or stained a natural color. Remember: Be honest. Do not even try to make it look like brick; it is concrete!

An organic house should virtually design itself. All one must do is ask the right questions and follow the logical conclusions. What is the watertable and how does it affect our design? Can we cover the home with earth, or should we only partially berm? What local building materials are available — stone and hemlock? Conclusion, we build a bermed structure of stone and hemlock.

Where does the sun shine? Where does the wind blow? We are confronted with a rugged site strewn with boulders and dotted with clusters of old oaks. We terrace downhill, placing our home among and around mighty trees and giant rocks.

The organic home is simple. It uses only a few materials, and it uses them honestly. We design the house on a module for structural and design uniformity. Elevations reflect the module in its glass and post placements. The smallest detail reflects the whole, and the whole is related to each part. The house is easy on the eye.

The colors are natural and healing. The spaces are proportioned to the human body; cabinets are designed so that short as well as tall persons can conveniently use them. The organic house is naturally warm in the winter and cool in the summer. It relates compatibly with its setting, both wild and man-made.

All this and more is what I have tried to accomplish in the designs in this book. I welcome dialogue and discussion on these ideas, and I sincerely hope I have not offended architects and homeowners with these frank remarks. However, I hope I have stirred their thought processes, for what I have written I firmly believe to be the truth.

Organic Rock House

Perspective

Organic Rock House

Description

The rock house was inspired by the great German architect of free form design, Eric Mendelsohn. To build such a structure today would probably be either cost prohibitive or simply a labor of love. This plan and rendering was developed in 1974 and is based on creating a structure that not only follows the contour of the land, but also utilizes natural materials found near the building site.

**Approx. 3200 Sq. Ft.
Custom plans only**

Floor Plan

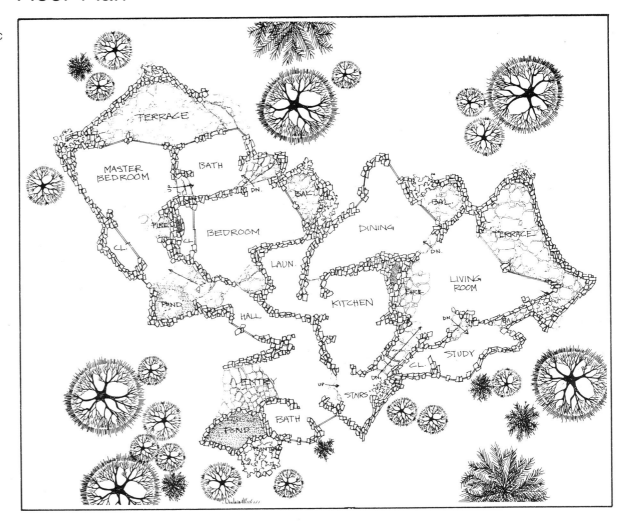

Free Form Jagged Rock

Perspective

Free Form Jagged Rock

Description

    Similar in design principle to the Organic Rock House, this stimulating imaginary organic residence is compatible with the surrounding site in which it is built—i.e., trees, rocks, slopes, etc. This type of house is quite viable structurally. Designed with straight walls rather than curved, it makes the concrete pours, insulating and waterproofing easier. It has south facing glass, exposed wood beams and stone facing on the exterior walls. Individual room privacy is gained by the offsetting hallway that stretches from the living area to the master bedroom.

Approx. 1700 Sq. Ft.
Custom plans only

Free Form Jagged Rock

Floor Plan

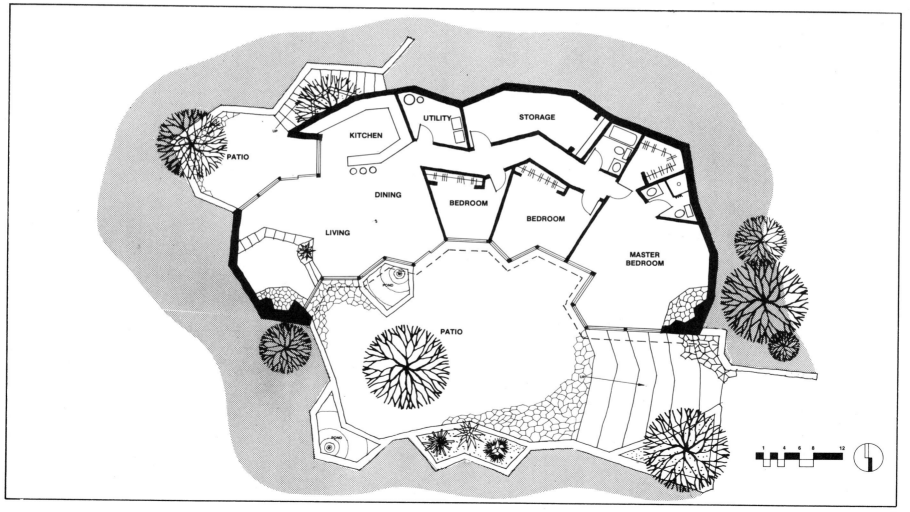

Cliff House

Description

Designed for a client but never built, the Cliff House is another example of an organic design building integrated with the landscape. Curved shapes are exposed to exhibit the beauty of the natural materials that hide the rectilinear designed rooms. Quiet and active areas of the home are set well apart from one another, as is the garage, guest room and storage area. In analyzing the two separate living areas, one can readily see the potential for creating an exquisite duplex. This plan could also be suitable for a library, museum or office complex.

Approx. 5000 sq. ft.
Custom plans only

Perspective

Cliff House

Floor Plan

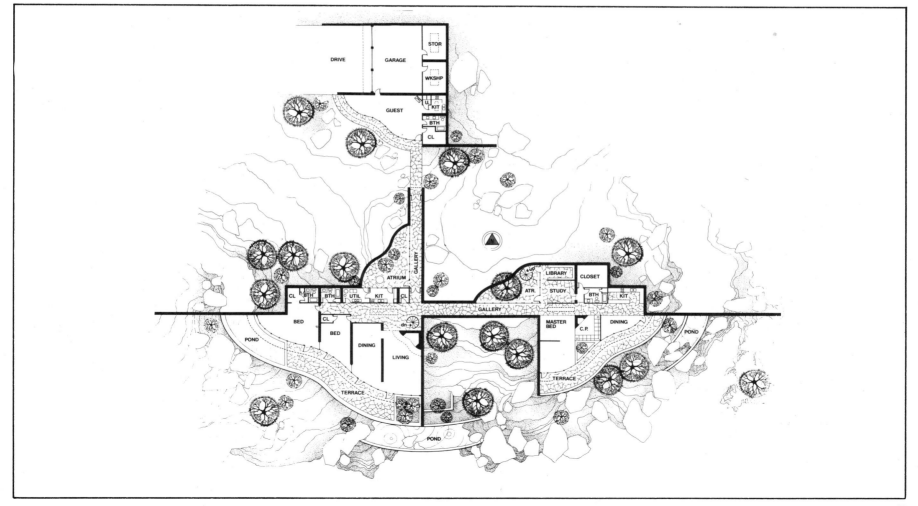

STOR

DRIVE   GARAGE

WKSHP

GUEST   U.   KIT

BTH

CL

GALLERY

ATRIUM

LIBRARY   CLOSET

ATR.   STUDY

BTH   KIT

CL   BTH   BTH   UTIL   KIT   CL   GALLERY

BED   CL   MASTER   C.P.   DINING

POND   BED   DINING   dn   BED   POND

LIVING   TERRACE

TERRACE

POND

The Pocono

Perspective

The Pocono

4

Description

 Imagine having the outdoors at your fingertips. This simple starter home offers the privacy of a spacious courtyard which could include a well landscaped pond or swimming pool. The proximity of the kitchen, bath, and utility room consolidate plumbing runs for even more dollar and space saving economy. Protected from the summer sun by a louvered overhang, the glazed front allows for ample natural light and passive solar gain. Flexibility is the key of this structure. Two bedrooms are featured, one of which could double as a working studio. Interior walls are adaptable to changing lifestyles and could be relocated. They are all non load bearing. (This house was designed for the Popular Science Home Plan Series, and appeared in the Sept. 1981 issue.)

1650 Sq. Ft.
Plans available

9

Floor Plan

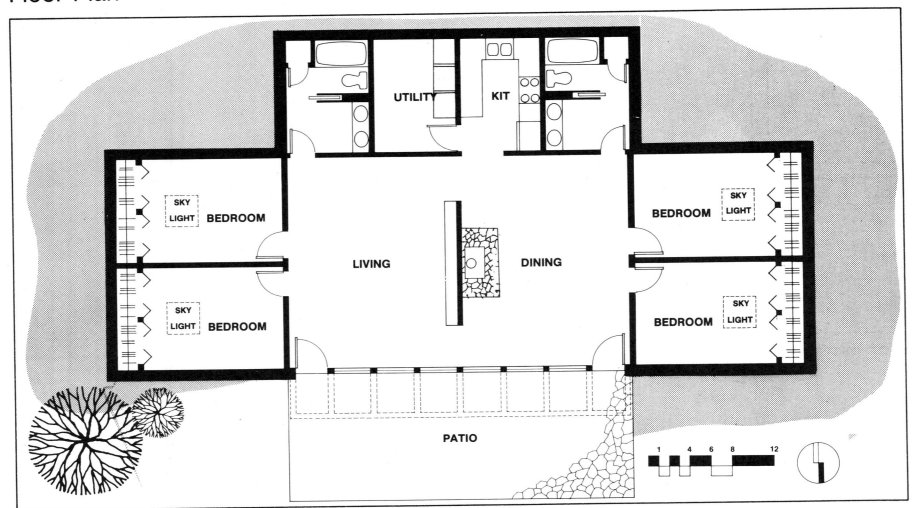

Ken Wilber's Hermitage

Perspective

PADORR-BLACK
82

Section

Description

Designed for my friend, Ken Wilber, East meets West in this orient-inspired residence which doubles as a heating and cooling experiment. By having both courtyards sunken to break the wind and having the greenhouse buffer zones facing east and west, it is believed the design could still become 50% or more efficient, especially when using insulated drapes. Solar panels on a berm next to the garage are there to assist, if needed. A wood beamed ceiling and skylights on each side of the massive stone fireplaces bring the many attributes of nature indoors.

1840 Sq. Ft.
3312 Sq. Ft. with greenhouses
Plans available

Floor Plan

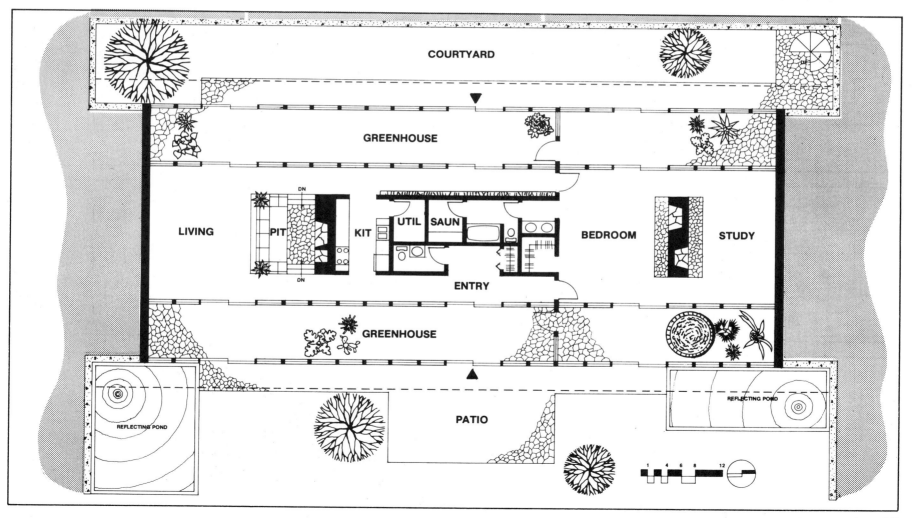

COURTYARD

GREENHOUSE

LIVING   PIT   KIT   UTIL   SAUN   BEDROOM   STUDY

DN

DN

ENTRY

GREENHOUSE

REFLECTING POND

REFLECTING POND

PATIO

1   4   6   8   12

Cashin Residence

6

Perspective

Rendering by Dennis Blair, architect

Cashin Residence

Description

An extremely practical structure, the Cashin residence was built in 1981 for a square foot cost slightly under that of surrounding above-grade homes. Designed for the suburbs, the terne-metal roof and angled earth berms present a home that does not conflict with those in the neighborhood that were conventionally built. Sunlight streams into the bedrooms and living spaces that exit onto a landscaped patio incorporating deciduous trees that give protection from the summer sun. Designed with Architect Dennis Blair.

2100 Sq. Ft.
Plans available

Floor Plan

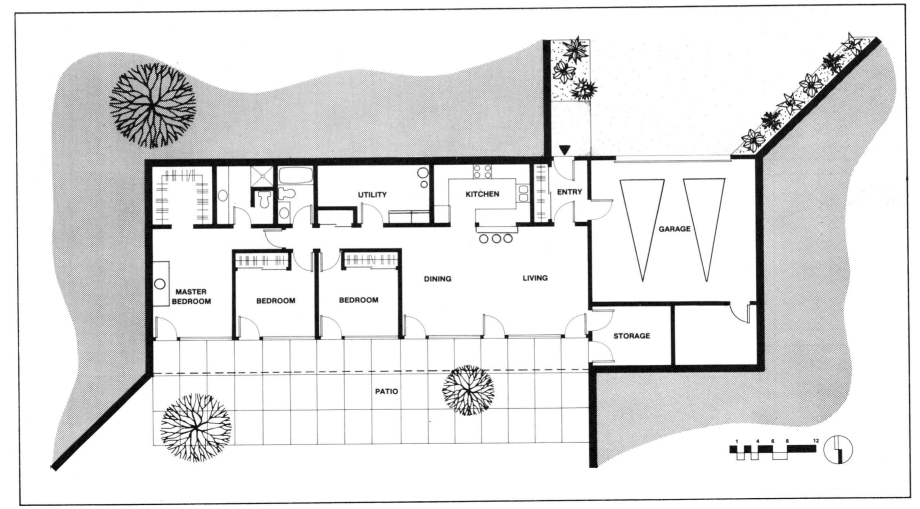

MASTER
BEDROOM

BEDROOM

BEDROOM

UTILITY

KITCHEN

ENTRY

DINING

LIVING

GARAGE

STORAGE

PATIO

1 4 6 8 12

Pyramid

Perspective

Pyramid

7

Description

Fashioned after the great pyramids of
El Giza, this home has three sunken courtyards
and a closed interior atrium allowing its
owners to see the clouds and birds drift
overhead and to watch the seasons change.
There is no lack of natural light in this plan; it is
open on all four sides. Inside, one can view the
entire house from one corner to the other. The
house has greenhouse buffer zones on the
north, east and west sides. Plan influenced
by architect Dennis Blair's atrium design houses.

2370 Sq. Ft.
Plans available

Floor Plan

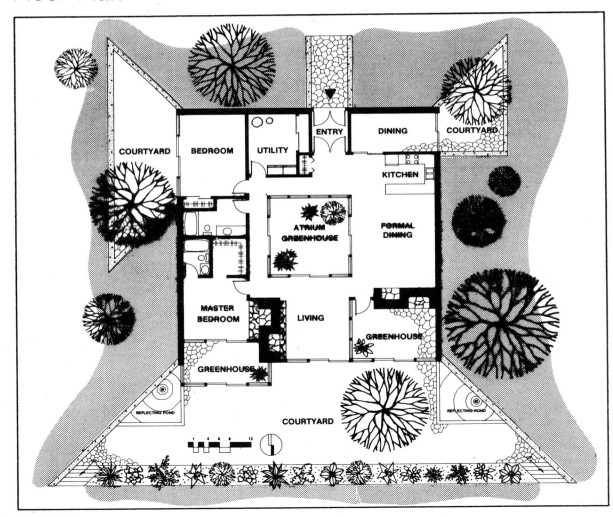

18

Perspective

Section

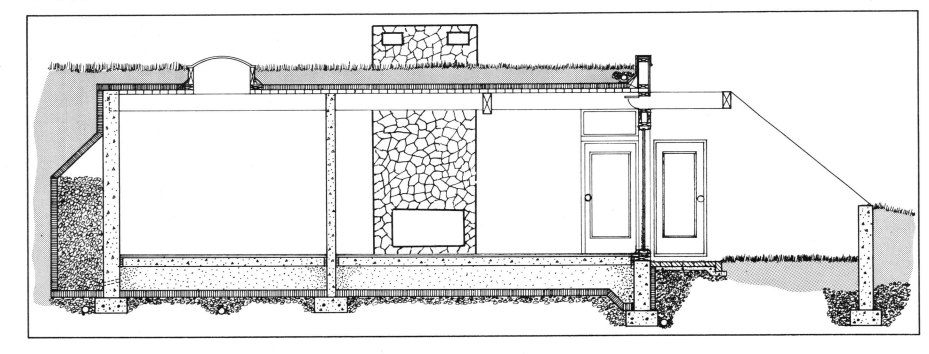

South Face I

Description

Many energy considerations were incorporated into this 1977 design emphasizing thermal mass. Ample passive gain penetrates the windows separating the living area and outside sunken courtyard, as well as attached greenhouse. All structures in the South Face series feature either poured or concrete block walls for mass and wood ceiling beams on four foot modules. This useful, compact plan offers an excellent southerly view. The greenhouse off the bedrooms provides additional depth to each room and additional living areas.

2000 Sq. Ft.
Plans available

Floor Plan

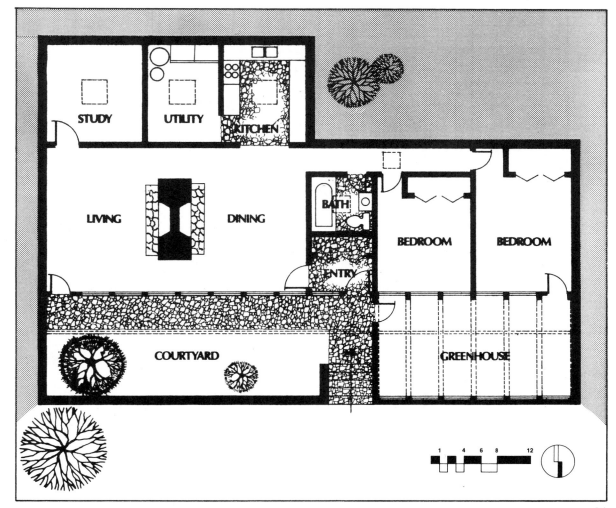

South Face II

Perspective

South Face II

Description

A sunken courtyard offers many advantages in areas where there is no view and private living space is desired. In extremely noisy areas, such as those surrounding airports, it also acts as a sound buffer. With the sunken courtyard eliminated and earth bermed retaining walls added at each end of the house, this basic L shaped design could connect, with a little imagination, into a home with a beautiful view. In a house orientated to the south, light would penetrate the family area in the morning and into the bedrooms with the afternoon and evening sun.

1840 Sq. Ft.
Plans available

Floor Plan

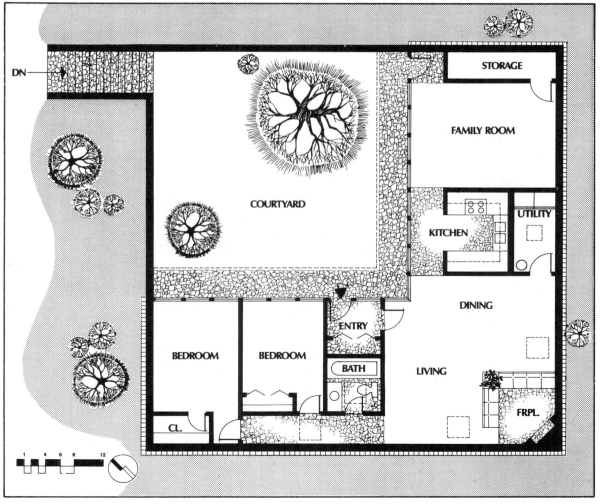

South Face III

Perspective

South Face III

Description

A larger variation of South Face I, this more luxurious version utilizes the wing walls to accent and separate the active and quiet areas of the home. Masonry floors are utilized throughout to store solar heat. Designed in four foot modules, it gives the builder plenty of flexibility in fitting the personal needs of the occupant to the interior space. A sunken courtyard off the living areas of this modern three bedroom plan, doubles as an attractive entryway.

3000 Sq. Ft.
Plans available

South Face III

10

Floor Plan

Elevation

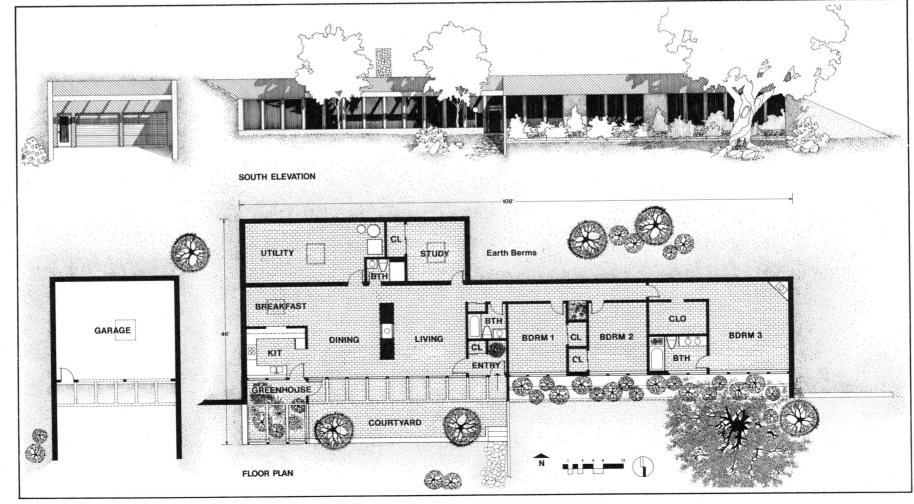

SOUTH ELEVATION

FLOOR PLAN

26

South Face IV

Perspective

Description

An expanded version of South Face I, this plan becomes an economical three bedroom solar assisted home. The master bedroom has a sunken patio and adjoins the greenhouse which is shared by two smaller bedrooms. Horizontal cedar or redwood siding meets the louvered overhangs to block out the hot summer sun.

2000 Sq. Ft.
Plans available

Floor Plan

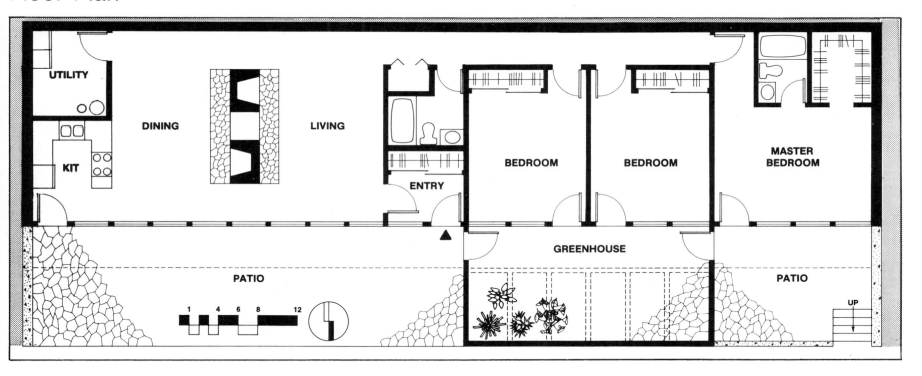

Covered Gable

Perspective

Covered Gable

Description

Designed with the suburb in mind, this attractive model provides its occupants with an environment to be envied. Inside, a cathedral beamed ceiling with tongue and groove planks catches the eye as you enter from a recessed patio. All three bedrooms have access to a greenhouse-patio combination that opens onto a recessed side yard. Stained cedar siding applied to the overhang accents this modern earth shelter home.

2320 Sq. Ft.
Plans available

Floor Plan

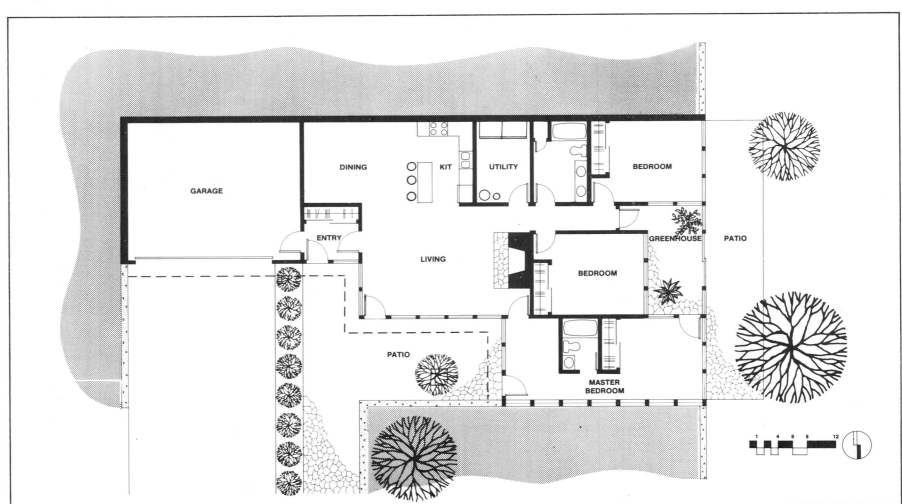

GARAGE

DINING

KIT

UTILITY

BEDROOM

ENTRY

LIVING

GREENHOUSE

PATIO

BEDROOM

PATIO

MASTER
BEDROOM

1 4 6 8 12

Earth Sheltered Arc

Perspective

Description

      This plan is ideally suited for, but not limited to, the top of a knoll or hill. Its semi-circle design not only presents a multi-directional viewing area, but allows the sunlight to enter the home from early morning until sunset. This house should be relatively easy and economical to build, utilizing a straight line retaining wall for the rear of the structure and curved outside walls consisting of facets of glass. The walls, floor, roof and parapet are reinforced concrete, exposed aggregate and ribbed. A see through fireplace separates a spacious dining and living room area from a conversation pit.

2200 Sq. Ft.
Custom plans only

Floor Plan

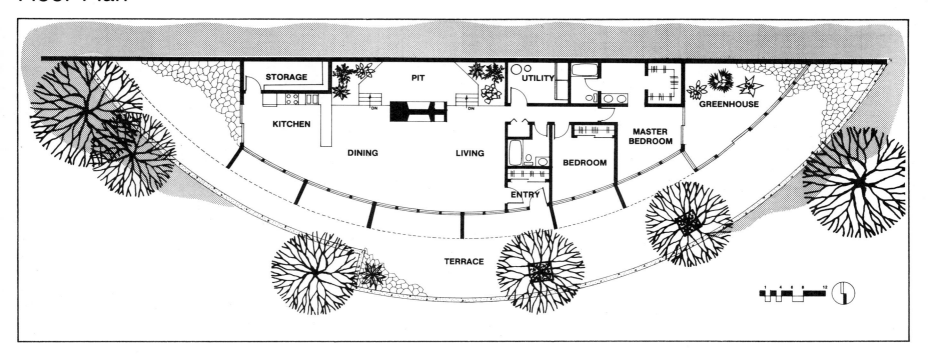

STORAGE

PIT

UTILITY

GREENHOUSE

KITCHEN

DINING

LIVING

MASTER BEDROOM

BEDROOM

ENTRY

TERRACE

Perspective

The Energy House

Description

The combination of berming to the roof line, creating air locks in the greenhouse and front entryway, and an R-63 thermal roof, creates a home that uses almost zero heating energy. Thermal mass storage of heat collected through the south facing greenhouse equipped with insulated drapes does the trick. A wood stove comes through for backup heat if needed. Conventional building materials and techniques are employed throughout.

2175 Sq. Ft.
Plans available

Floor Plan

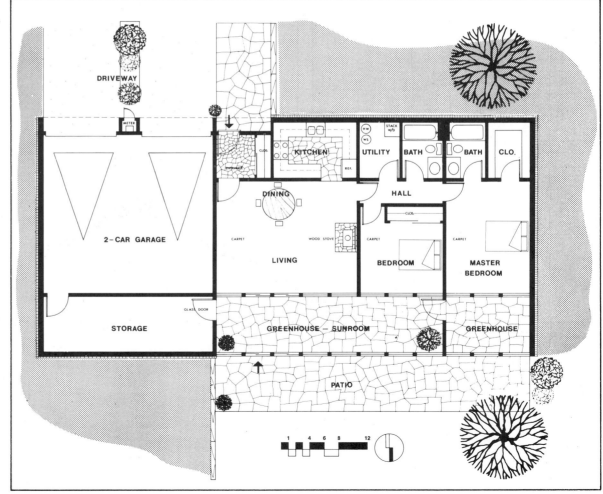

Elevation

Section

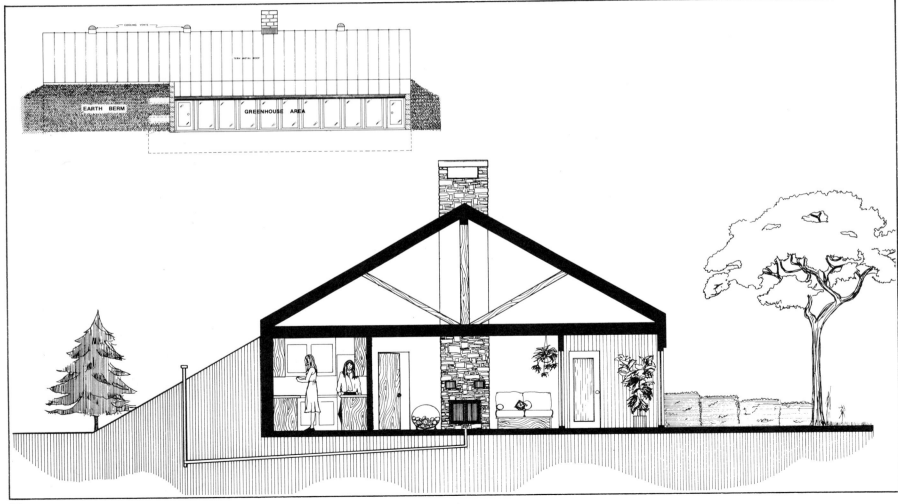

Perspective

Section

Description

This versatile, module, passive solar home can be enlarged or reduced according to family size or budget. The garage and studio on the north are separated from the house by a courtyard that provides both light and a social gathering area. Clerestory windows let the sunlight stream into the kitchen, bath and master bedrooms.

A greenhouse, acting as a solar collecting room, has thermal mass designed into the storage wall. Three feet of rock storage lay beneath the insulated concrete floor slab. Other solar collection points are the house's R-32 insulated concrete wall and R-15 floors, and a massive masonry fireplace. Construction materials include a wood plank and beam truss R-48 roof, capped with metal roofing. Backup heat for this energy efficient passive solar home is by hot water radiant heating in the floor's slabs. The plan can be built into a hillside or on a grade.

2500 Sq. Ft.
Plans available

Elevation

Section

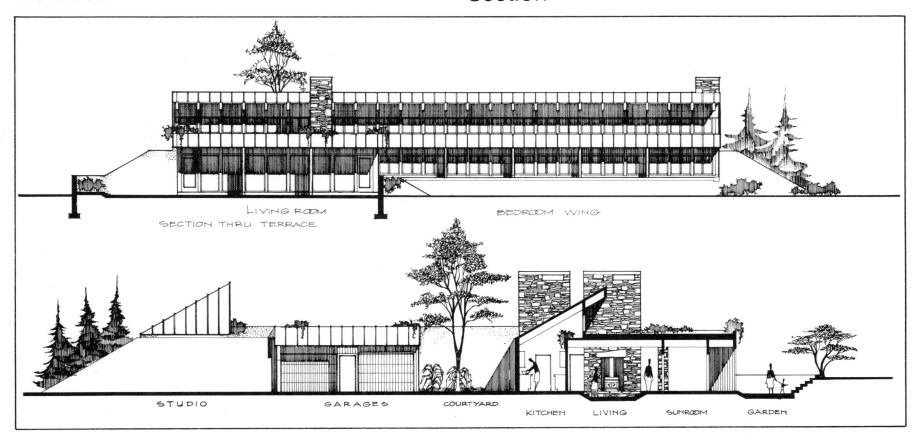

LIVING ROOM
SECTION THRU TERRACE

BEDROOM WING

STUDIO · GARAGES · COURTYARD · KITCHEN · LIVING · SUNROOM · GARDEN

Floor Plan

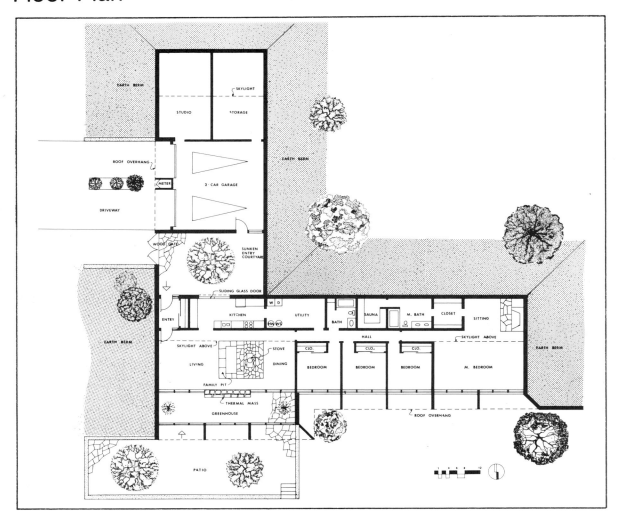

Bermed T

Perspective

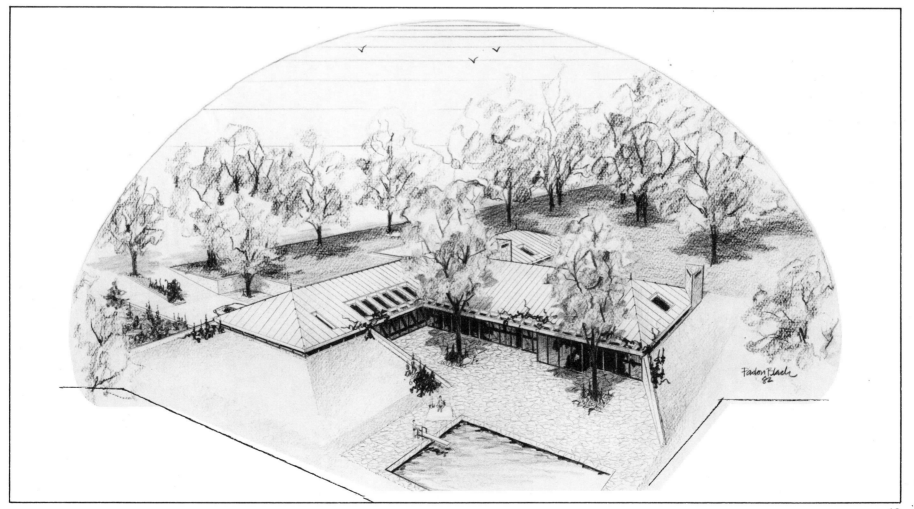

Bermed T

Description

This earth shelter is destined for any street in any community. The lines of the low angled berms are continued on the seamed lines of the terne metal roof. The conventional thermal roof covers a very basic, spacious floor plan. Inspired by Frank Lloyd Wright's bermed Usonia houses, this home incorporates attached garage, greenhouse, sunken courtyard and various stone covered fireplaces. All sleeping areas have two exits to meet egress codes.

3070 Sq. Ft.
Plans available

Bermed T

Floor Plan

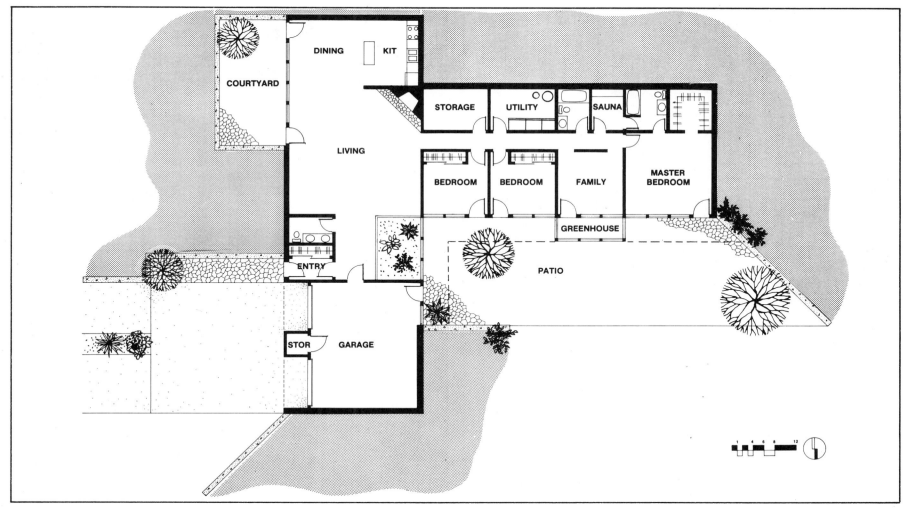

COURTYARD

DINING   KIT

STORAGE   UTILITY   SAUNA

LIVING

BEDROOM   BEDROOM   FAMILY   MASTER BEDROOM

GREENHOUSE

ENTRY

PATIO

STOR   GARAGE

Hermit Cabin

Perspective

Hermit Cabin

Description

Under 600 sq. ft., this small hermitage is an ideal retreat for a writer, woodsperson, or just for weekends away from the hectic city life. This simple modular plan offers low cost construction using concrete block or poured walls, a slab floor and open wood beam ceiling that contains a skylight. A greenhouse, with a stone floor for heat storage, expands the dining and kitchen area. The living room converts into a bedroom at night with a pull-down Murphy bed. A warm fire in the wood stove provides back up heat and will take the chill off during the evening hours. Ideal for the self-builder!

550 Sq. Ft.
Plans available

Floor Plan

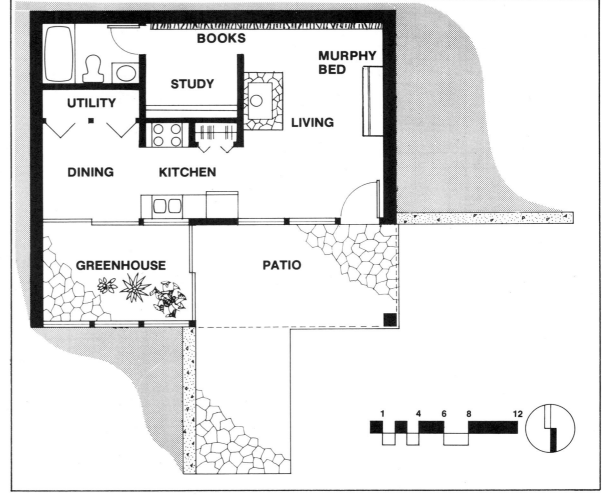

BOOKS

MURPHY BED

STUDY

UTILITY

LIVING

DINING

KITCHEN

GREENHOUSE

PATIO

1   4   6   8   12

Pyramid Cottage

Description

A small but elegant, yet affordable, cottage has long been sought by earth shelter enthusiasts. Positioned toward the south, the living areas fill with sunlight which is buffered through the corner greenhouse. A sofa or murphy bed converts the living space into a bedroom in the evening. A super-insulated thermal roof makes this compact plan almost 100% energy efficient.

676 Sq. Ft.
Plans available

Perspective

Section

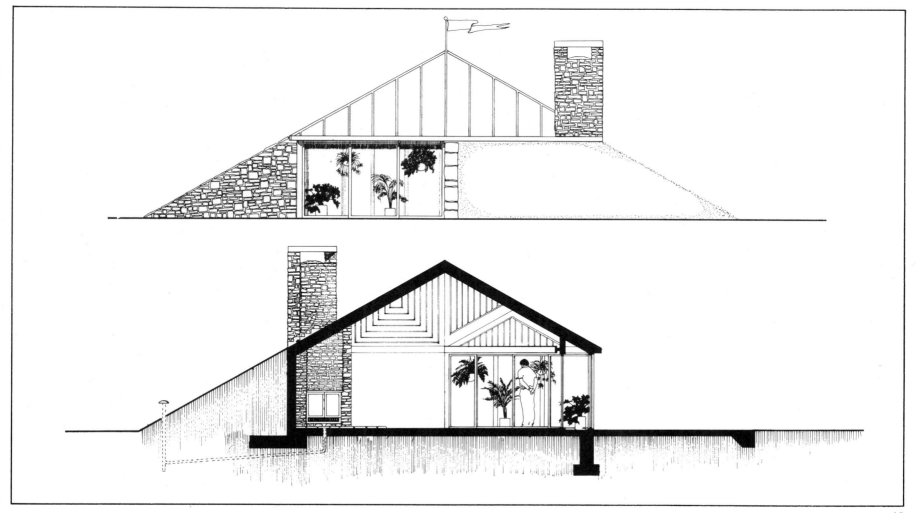

Floor Plan

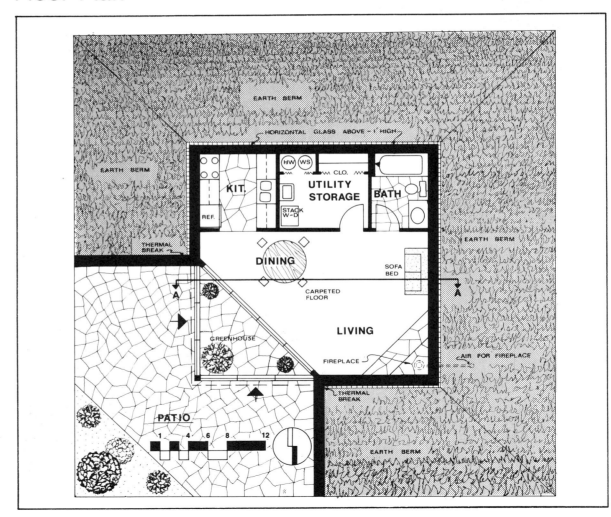

Sloped Roof Cabin

Perspective

Description

Designed to be a small, economic starter home, the sloped-roof cabin is built by utilizing either concrete block or poured concrete walls, concrete slab and post, plank and beam south wall and wood construction. The economy of this design is due, in part, to the use of a super-insulated thermal roof instead of covering the home with earth. An R-48 insulated roof reduces heat loss. Built on a four foot module, simple building techniques are used throughout.

936 Sq. Ft.
Plans available

Section

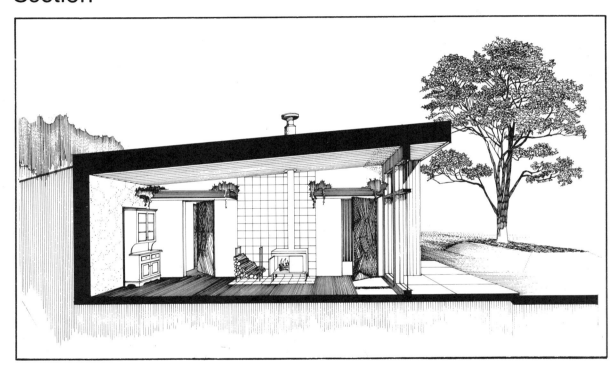

Floor Plan

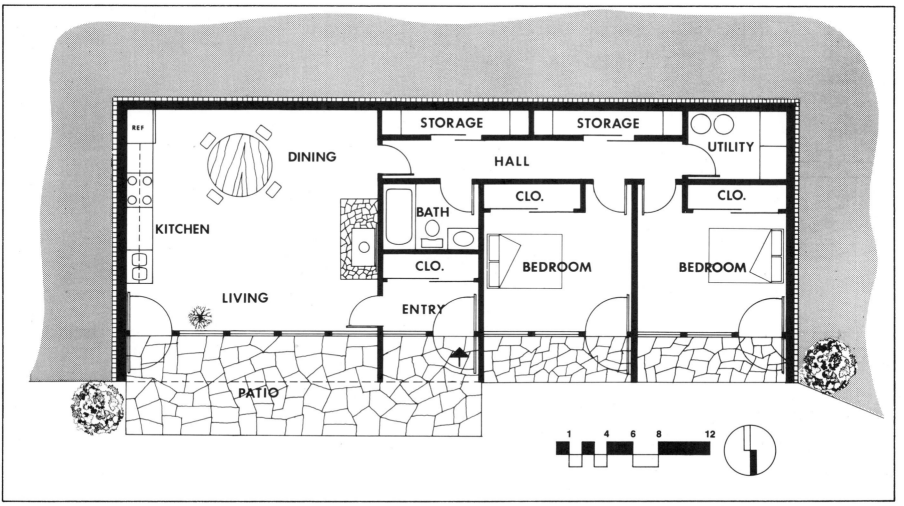

Perspective

Basic Passive Module

Description

Designed in 1980 for the Popular Science "Leisure Home Plan" series, this home drew the largest response in the 10-year history of that monthly feature. Inspired by the famous architect Mies van der Rohe's courtyard designs, the extensive use of glass brings an elegant look to this low cost house. It is built in modules with no interior load bearing walls (as are a number of homes in this plan book) permitting the interior floor plan to be redesigned in the future. A wood burning stove provides backup heat for this already energy efficient home.

1100 Sq. Ft.
Plans available

Basic Passive Module

Interior Perspective

Elevation

Section

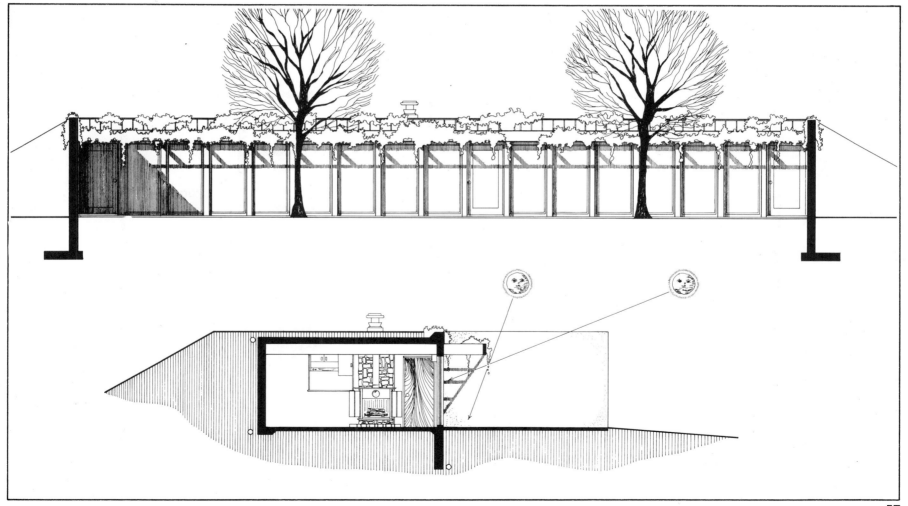

Floor Plan

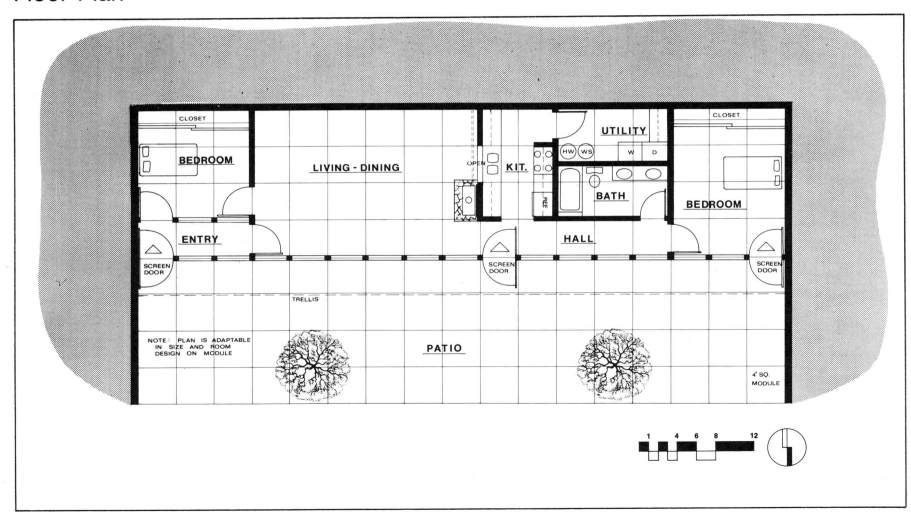

CLOSET

BEDROOM

LIVING - DINING

OPEN

KIT.

UTILITY

W   D

HW WS

CLOSET

BEDROOM

REF

BATH

ENTRY

HALL

SCREEN DOOR

SCREEN DOOR

SCREEN DOOR

TRELLIS

NOTE: PLAN IS ADAPTABLE IN SIZE AND ROOM DESIGN ON MODULE

PATIO

4' SQ. MODULE

1   4   6   8   12

Perspective

Suburban Builder

Description

A combination of bermed wall, thermal roof and clerestory windows bring light well into the recessed rooms in the rear of the home, making this structure of particular interest to the average contractor and developer. Buffered greenhouses along the south facing front are accessible from the living room and each of the bedrooms, expanding the living space considerably. A convenient shop and storage area in the back of the garage works out well for the family handyman. Excess heat from solar gain is stored in the greenhouse floor.

3330 Sq. Ft.
Plans available

Section

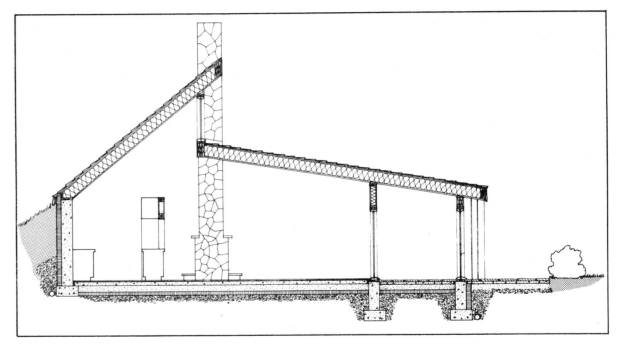

Floor Plan

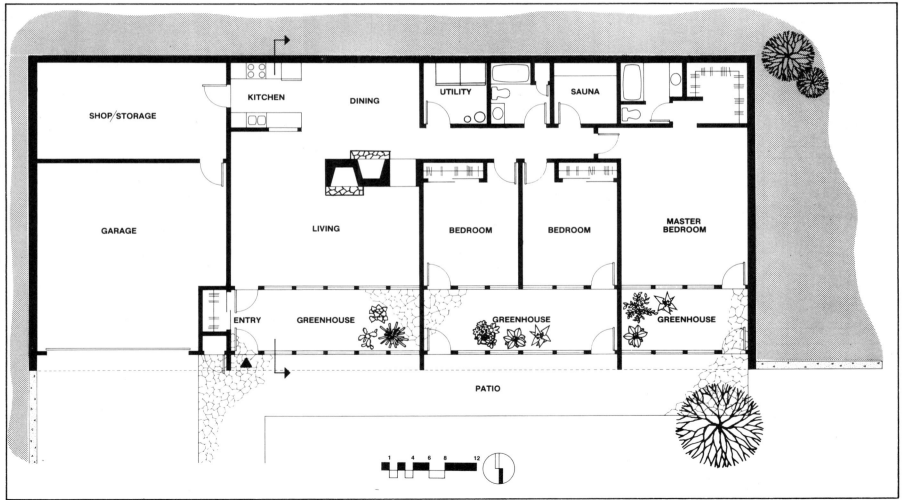

SHOP/STORAGE

KITCHEN

DINING

UTILITY

SAUNA

GARAGE

LIVING

BEDROOM

BEDROOM

MASTER BEDROOM

ENTRY

GREENHOUSE

GREENHOUSE

GREENHOUSE

PATIO

1 4 6 8 12

V-Wing

Perspective

V-Wing

Description

The rectilinear profile of this home creates a natural openness; yet it can become very private. Sliding glass doors lend an expansive aura inside to the outdoor masonry patio that houses a bank of solar panels. Poured concrete walls and a joist roof can make this house both cost effective and energy efficient. It can be tucked away very neatly onto either a suburban lot or rural acreage.

3200 Sq. Ft.
Plans available

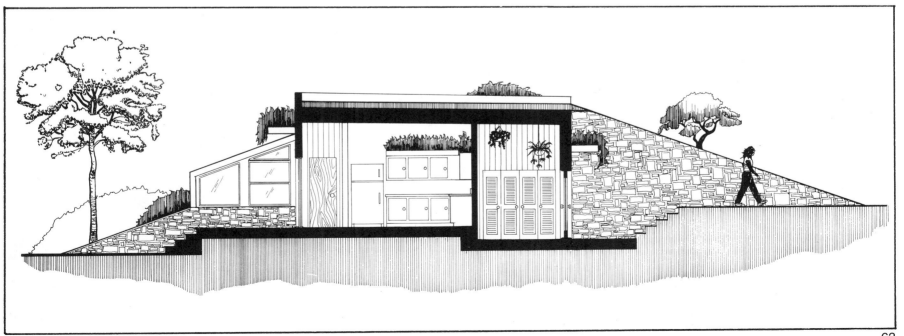

Floor Plan

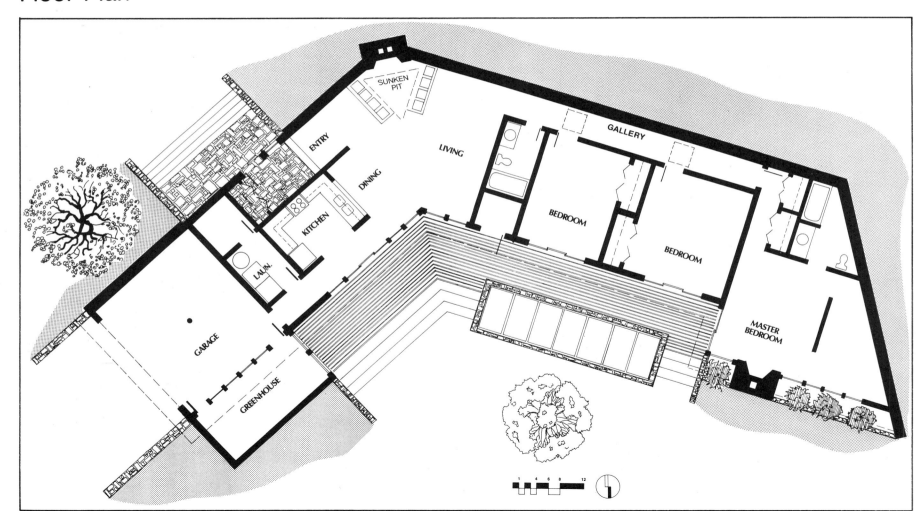

SUNKEN PIT

ENTRY

GALLERY

LIVING

DINING

KITCHEN

BEDROOM

BEDROOM

LAUN.

GARAGE

MASTER BEDROOM

GREENHOUSE

1 4 6 8 12

Passive Wing

Perspective

Passive Wing

Description

Among the many features available for the right family are an angled floor plan, solar greenhouse, beamed ceiling and sunken courtyards. The wing shape gives privacy and allows light into all areas of the house. The quiet sleeping areas are away from the formal dining and living room. If the floor plan is suitable but the square footage excessive, it could be reduced by shrinking the area between the kitchen and the family room.

4000 Sq. Ft.
Plans available

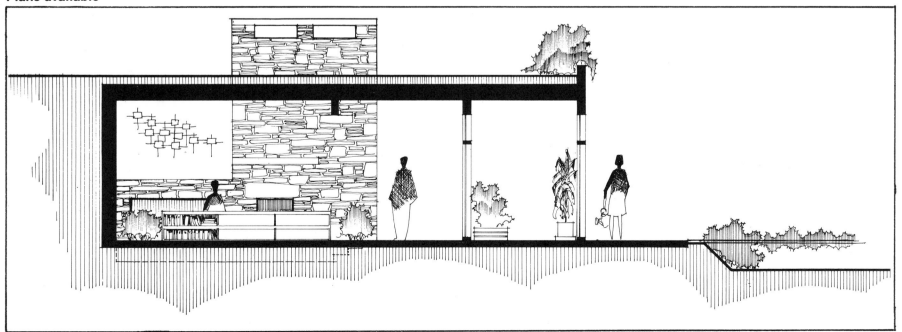

Passive Wing

Floor Plan

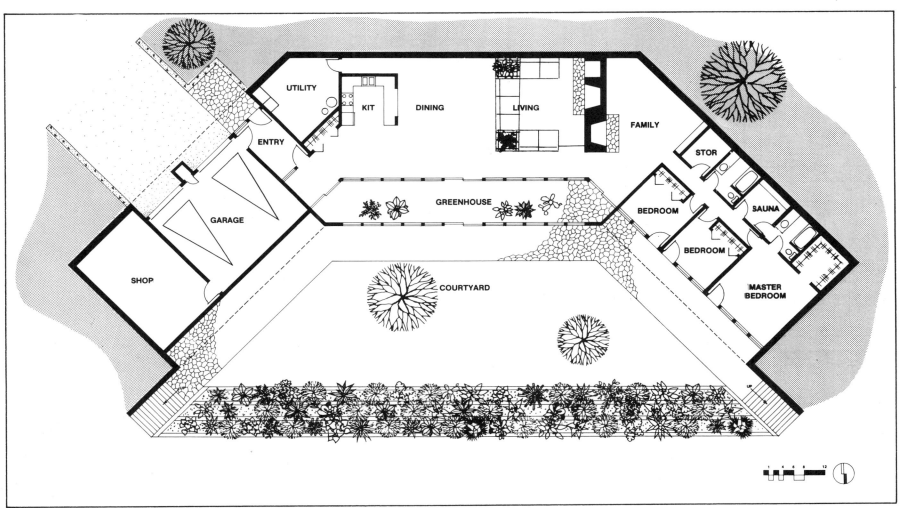

U-Shaped House

Perspective

U-Shaped House

Description

Hidden from view in the rendering is a very private courtyard which surrounds a full size swimming pool and has access from any room in the house. A formal dining area adjoins a spacious living room, separated by a large see-through fireplace. Large and luxurious, this house is for the discerning executive.

2350 Sq. Ft.
Plans available

Section

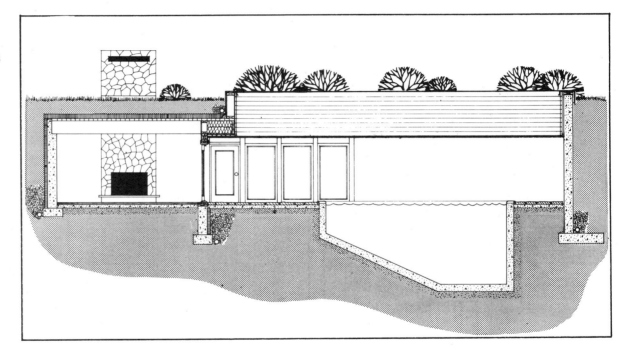

Floor Plan

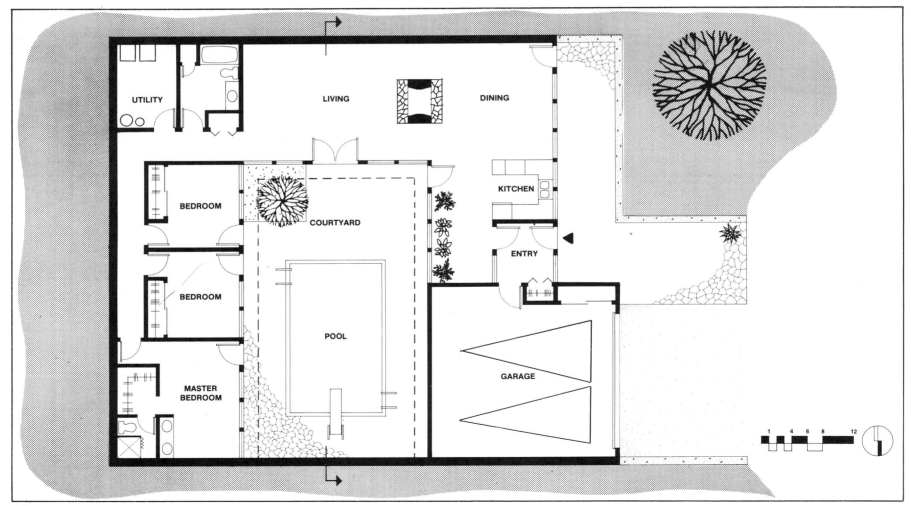

Perspective

H-Wedge

Description

Perhaps one of the best examples of blending organic architecture with the environment may be found in this H-Wedge design. Not only does it work well as a residential structure, but it also could be expanded and adapted to a commercial application. The long sloping angles of the berms carry up onto the roof and solar panels. The entrance offers a protective approach; yet by using glass it is light and airy. Living and sleeping areas are separated by a large formal entry, complete with decorative plants and benches. This setting is enhanced by a view into the courtyard located in the back of the structure.

2550 Sq. Ft.
Plans available

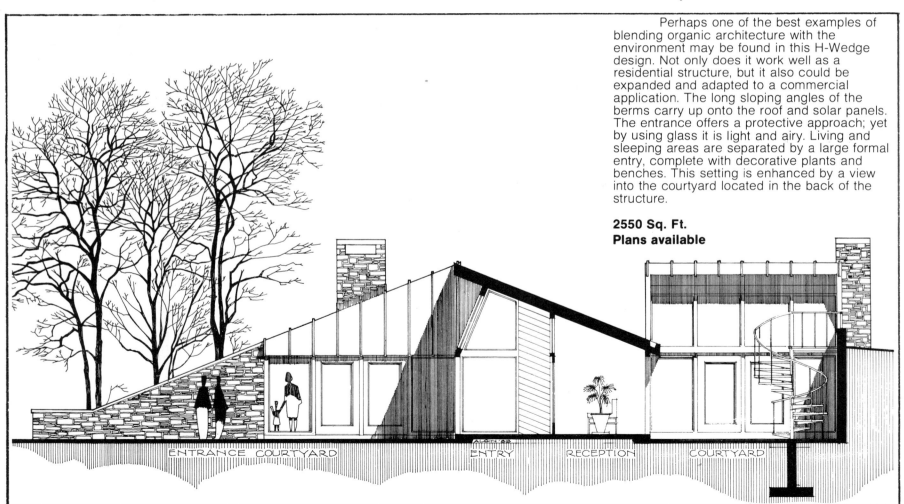

ENTRANCE COURTYARD   ENTRY   RECEPTION   COURTYARD

Floor Plan

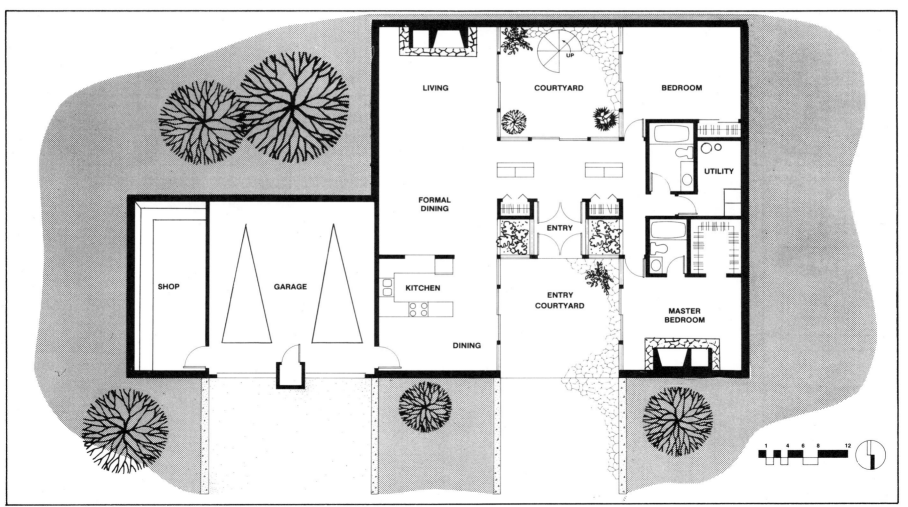

LIVING

COURTYARD

BEDROOM

UTILITY

FORMAL
DINING

ENTRY

SHOP

GARAGE

KITCHEN

ENTRY
COURTYARD

MASTER
BEDROOM

DINING

UP

1 4 6 8 12

Perspective

Country Courtyard

Section

Description

Recessed clerestory windows allow for the flooding of sunlight into this rambling home that surrounds a spacious patio. Gained heat is stored in the thermal mass on the concrete and stone floors and walls. An insulating shutter or curtain can be drawn across all windows, including those facing the courtyard, in the evening or winter to prevent heat loss. The structure is of post and beam construction, has few interior load bearing walls and is built in 12 foot sections. The courtyard is a four-season focal point and can be enjoyed from most rooms in this spacious plan. (This house was commissioned by Popular Science for its Leisure Home Plan series, and it appeared in the Sept. 1982 issue).

3500 Sq. Ft.
Plans available

Section

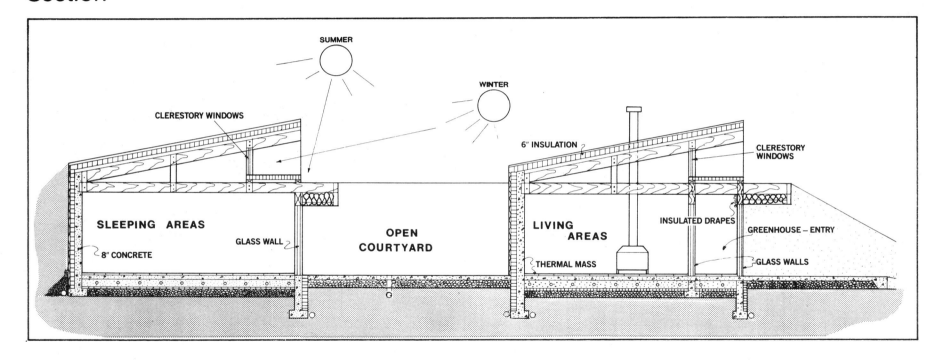

SUMMER

WINTER

CLERESTORY WINDOWS

6" INSULATION

CLERESTORY WINDOWS

SLEEPING AREAS

8" CONCRETE

GLASS WALL

OPEN COURTYARD

LIVING AREAS

THERMAL MASS

INSULATED DRAPES

GREENHOUSE – ENTRY

GLASS WALLS

Floor Plan

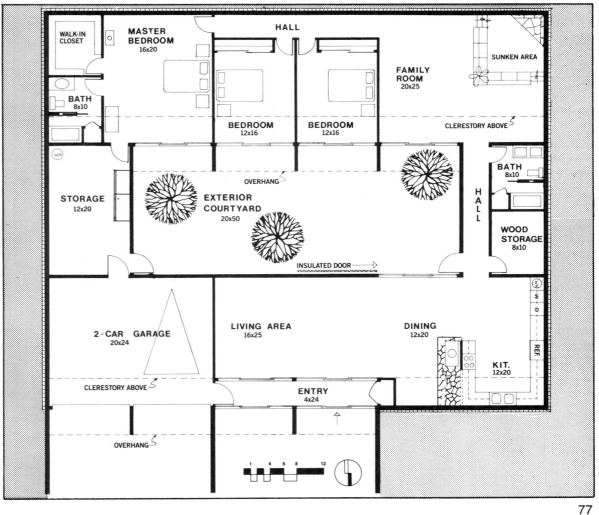

All Wood Home

Description

Designed to use economical all-wood foundation, walls, floor and roof, this structure is very easy to build, even in winter. A super-insulated ceiling is capped by a built-up tar and gravel roof, which if re-designed properly, could carry earth on top. Once the shell is in place, waterproofed and backfilled, the interior could be finished by those home owners with the appropriate skills to do so. An excellent plan for an affordable down sized starter or retirement home.

1130 Sq. Ft.
Plans available

Perspective

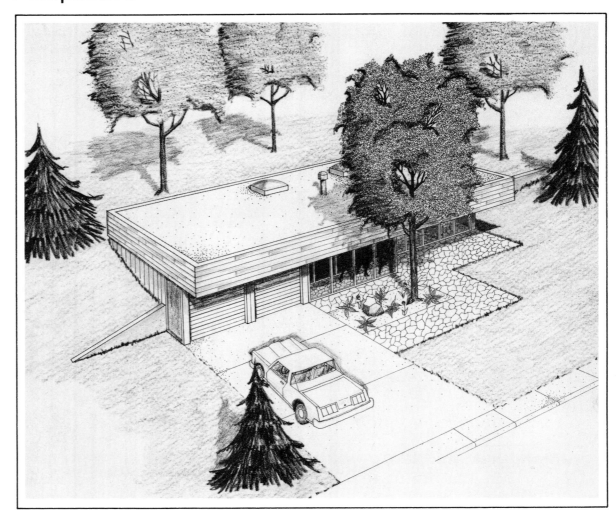

Floor Plan

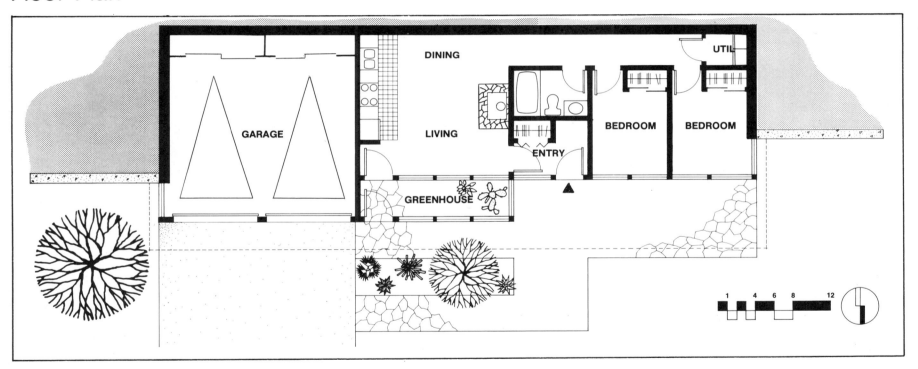

GARAGE

DINING

UTIL

LIVING

BEDROOM

BEDROOM

ENTRY

GREENHOUSE

1 4 6 8 12

Architerra

Description

A unique mix of rectilinear and curvilinear design, this plan for Architerra clearly shows how earth sheltered multiple housing can be stepped back into a hillside and blend softly with the environment.

Architerra is a totally new concept that is well suited for developing different sites where slope angles may vary from 25-45 degrees, where soil conditions may be poor or where restoration of stripped or eroded hillsides is required. The system uses an associated technology, Reinforced Earth©, to shape and stabilize the site and make construction possible on sites that were previously undevelopable.

The advantages of the Architerra concept are many. Besides being earth sheltered, which provides lower energy and maintenance costs, each unit has its own private patio off the living and sleeping areas that produces an aesthetically pleasing, landscaped appearance.

A 12 unit project is planned for Vail, Colorado. Charles G. Woods and Dennis Blair, designers. Dennis Blair, architect.

2300 Sq. Ft. per unit
Plans not available

Perspective

Perspective

Section

Floor Plan

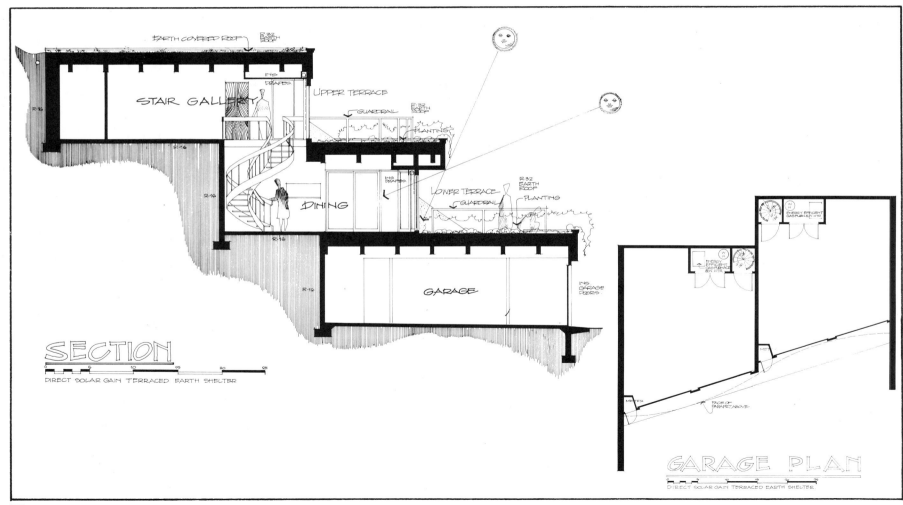

Floor Plan

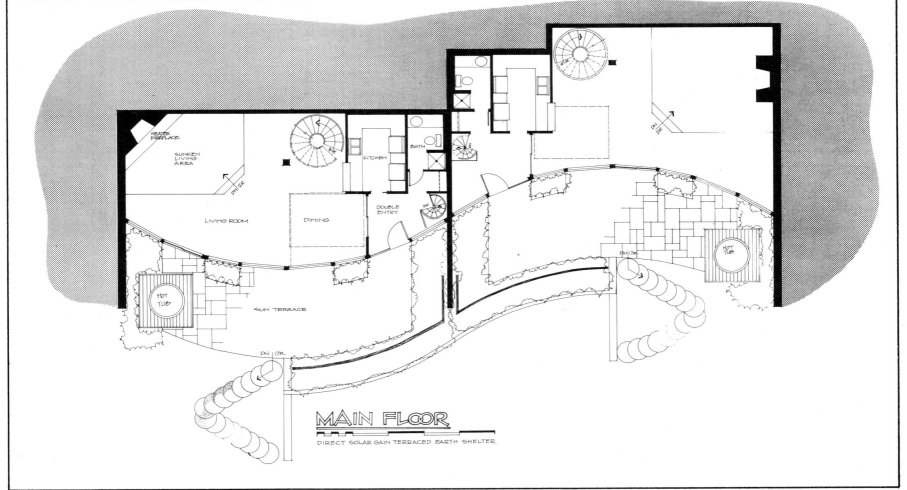

HEATER
FIREPLACE

SUNKEN
LIVING
AREA

KITCHEN

BATH

DN 12R

DOUBLE
ENTRY

DN

LIVING ROOM

DINING

HOT
TUB

SUN TERRACE

DN 17R

DN 17R

HOT
TUB

DN 17R

MAIN FLOOR

DIRECT SOLAR GAIN TERRACED EARTH SHELTER

Floor Plan

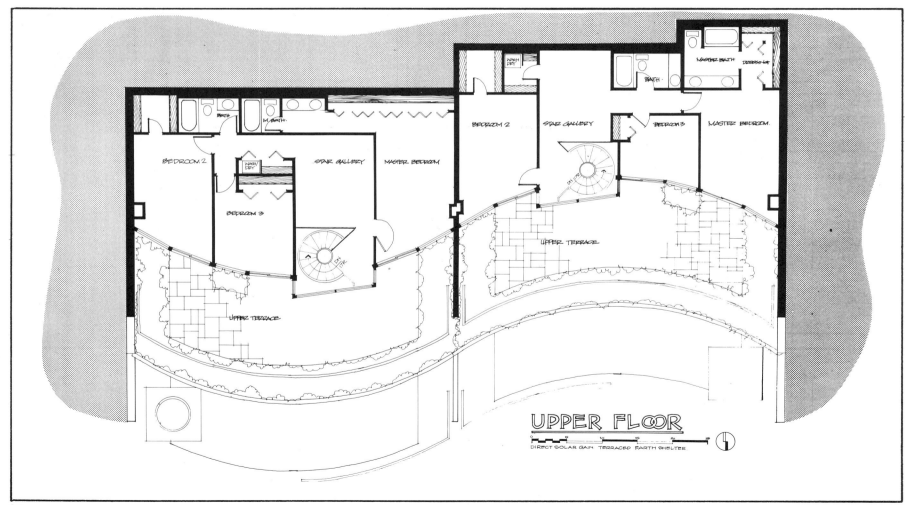

BEDROOM 2

BATH

M. BATH

STAIR GALLERY

MASTER BEDROOM

WASH/DRY

BEDROOM 3

UPPER TERRACE

WASH/DRY

BEDROOM 2

STAIR GALLERY

BATH

BEDROOM 3

MASTER BEDROOM

MASTER BATH

DRESSING

UPPER TERRACE

UPPER FLOOR

DIRECT SOLAR GAIN TERRACED EARTH SHELTER

Perspective

Description

Part fantasy! Part reality! The only feature lacking in this expensive mountain top design is a cable car. The Chateau definitely expands the scope of conventional housing into something other than basic rectilinear designs. All large bedroms have access to a large patio and pool. Sunlight enters the rear of the home through clerestory windows tucked beneath the curved terne metal roof. Construction costs would be more viable if this were kept to a one floor residence.

4700 Sq. Ft.
Custom plans only

Floor Plan

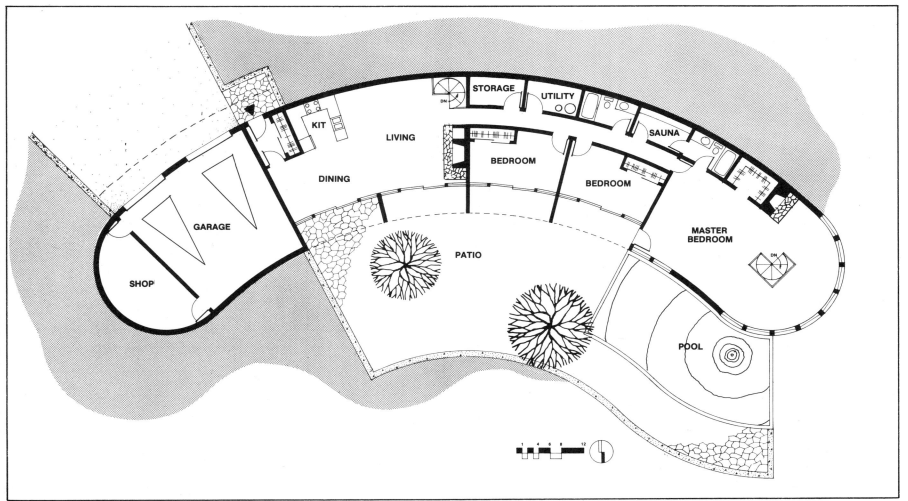

Perspective

Sawtooth Plan

Description

      Designed for a site where south is some degrees off the natural slope of the land, the Sawtooth Plan lends itself to a given direction when a certain view is desired. This home is suitable for southern climates to cut down on glass area and heat gain. For northern climates, it may be appropriate to glaze the entire south wall. Triangles developed by the Sawtooth design offer nice areas for planters. Built-up tar and gravel roofing covers the flat portion of the roof with a terne metal shed roof covering a bank of clerestory windows that let the sunlight down into the hallway.

2900 Sq. Ft.
Plans available

Sawtooth Plan

Elevation   Section

Floor Plan

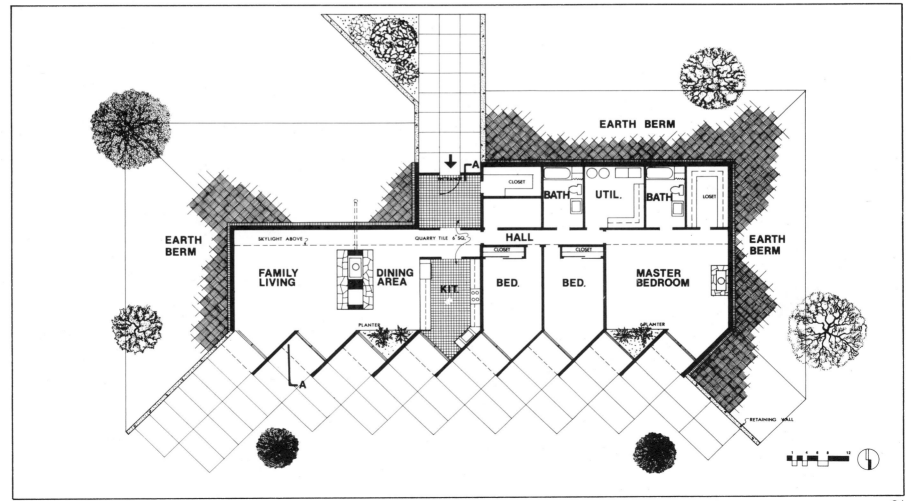

EARTH BERM

EARTH BERM

CLOSET

BATH UTIL. BATH LOSET

HALL

SKYLIGHT ABOVE QUARRY TILE 6" SQ.

EARTH BERM

EARTH BERM

CLOSET CLOSET

FAMILY LIVING DINING AREA KIT. BED. BED. MASTER BEDROOM

PLANTER PLANTER

RETAINING WALL

Perspective

Wopo and Peter House

Description

Designed to utilize the maximum direct solar gain, this open plan has closet space galore. The attractive geometric shaped metal roof costs more than asphalt but will last considerably longer. The house features built-in couches and book cases on each side of the fireplace, and a cantilevered 8-foot roof overhang.

1470 Sq. Ft.
Plans available

Interior Perspective

Wopo and Peter House

Elevation   Section

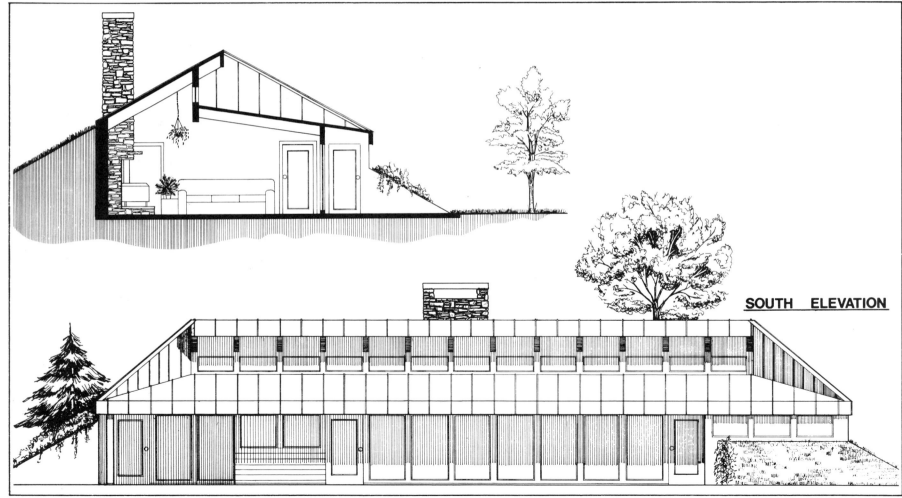

SOUTH ELEVATION

Wopo and Peter House

Floor Plan

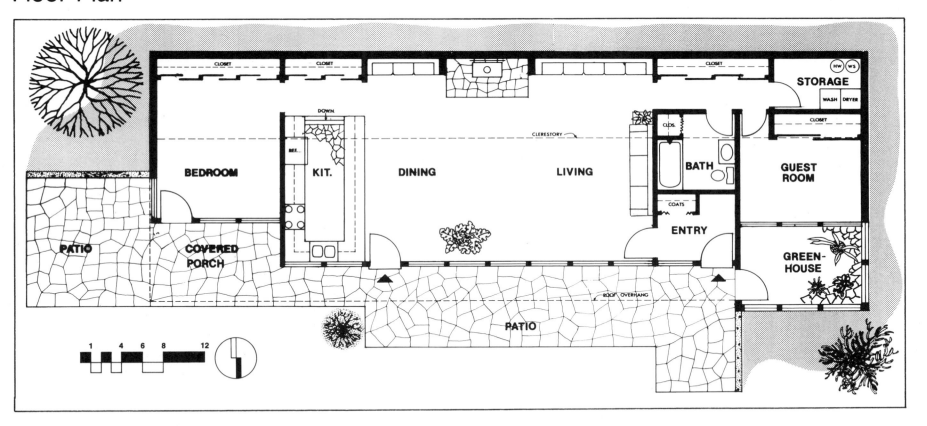

CLOSET
CLOSET
CLOSET
HW WS
STORAGE
WASH DRYER
CLOSET
DOWN
CLERESTORY
REF.
CLOS.
BEDROOM
KIT.
DINING
LIVING
BATH
GUEST ROOM
COATS
PATIO
COVERED PORCH
ENTRY
GREEN-HOUSE
ROOF OVERHANG
PATIO

1 4 6 8 12

St. Croix Estates

Description

This low-cost multiple unit townhouse or condominium shares common soundproof walls of concrete, with intermediate wood joist floors. Each bedroom and study have access to private balconies that offer a scenic view and at the same time allow ample sunlight to penetrate well into the recesses of each floor. An additional spiral staircase could be placed outside on the balconies providing a way to the courtyard on the roof. The elevational rendering shows the type of site on which the units could be constructed. Charles G. Woods and Dennis Blair, designers. Dennis Blair, architect.

2510 Sq. Ft. per unit
Plans not available

Perspective

Elevation

Floor Plan

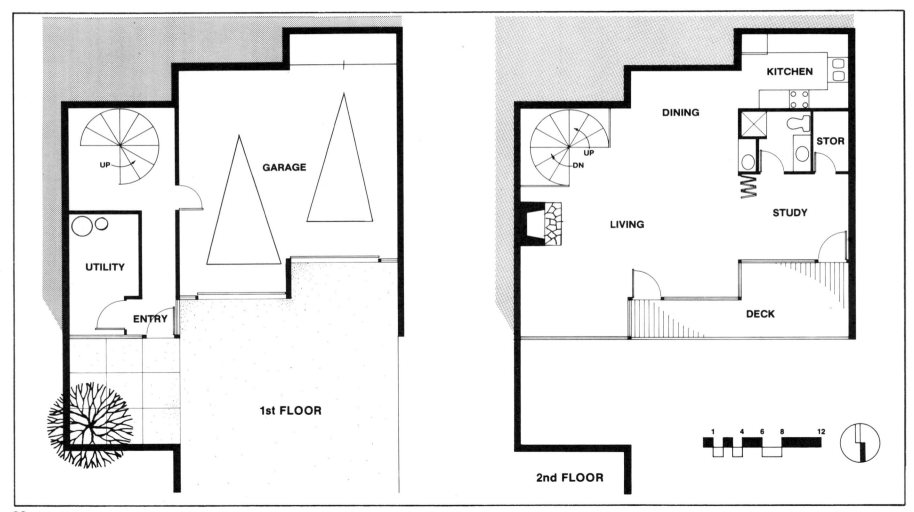

UP

GARAGE

UTILITY

ENTRY

1st FLOOR

KITCHEN

DINING

STOR

UP

DN

STUDY

LIVING

DECK

2nd FLOOR

1   4   6   8   12

Floor Plan

Section

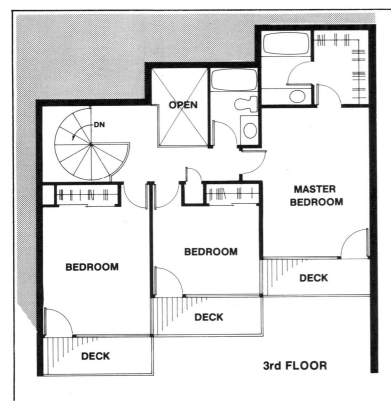

OPEN

DN

MASTER BEDROOM

BEDROOM

BEDROOM

DECK

DECK

DECK

3rd FLOOR

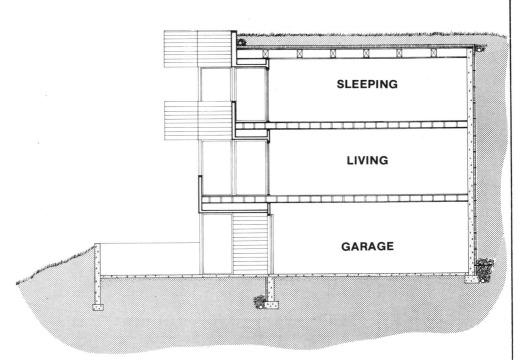

SLEEPING

LIVING

GARAGE

The Octagon

Perspective

Description

A very efficient, well thought out plan for those desiring an amply lighted home with many views to the east, south and west. Economy is built into this plan by the strategic placement of the baths, utility and kitchen permitting centralized plumbing runs. A sunken conversation pit, with fireplace separate the formal dining and living areas. Corner overhangs provide room for small trees and even a pond or two. This plan is very compact and opens to the spacious exterior patio which wraps itself around five sides of the octagon.

2000 Sq. Ft.
Plans available

Floor Plan

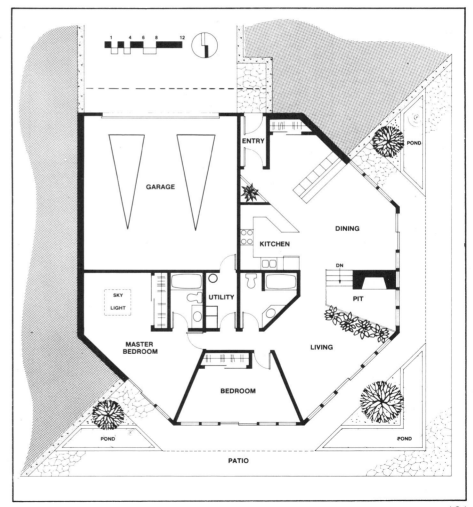

Perspective

Executive Condominium

Description

This luxurious condominium project offers a very spacious floor plan. The entry at the lower level adds privacy to the second and third floors. The second floor living area opens onto a beautiful stone terrace which can be used to entertain a large group of friends or business clients. Three bedrooms highlight the third floor with the master bedroom having its own sauna, walk-in closet, fireplace and private terrace. Construction methods used include reinforced concrete walls, concrete precast planks, and a well insulated wood shed roof on the third floor.

4000 Sq. Ft.
Custom plans only

Section

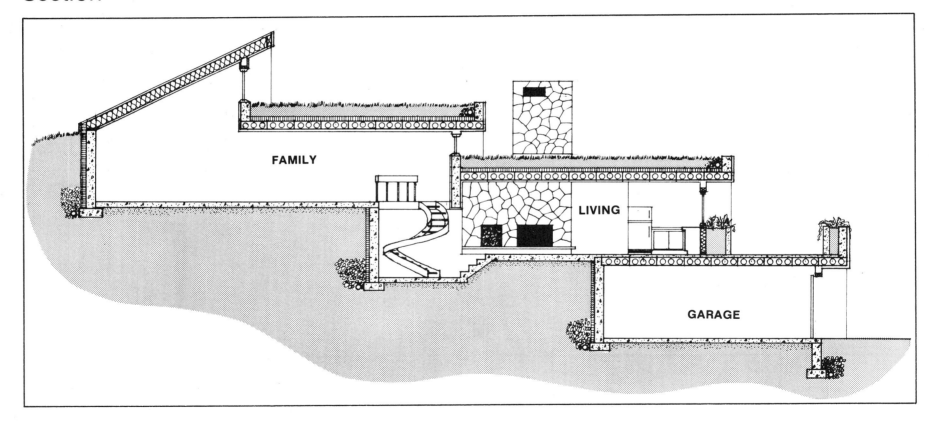

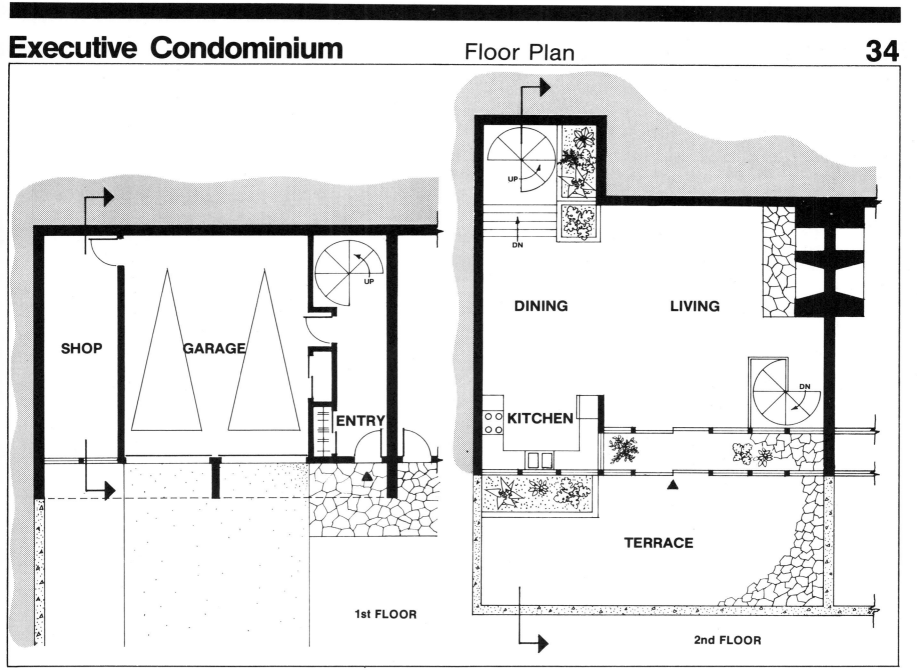

SHOP

GARAGE

UP

ENTRY

1st FLOOR

UP

DN

DINING

LIVING

KITCHEN

DN

TERRACE

2nd FLOOR

Floor Plan

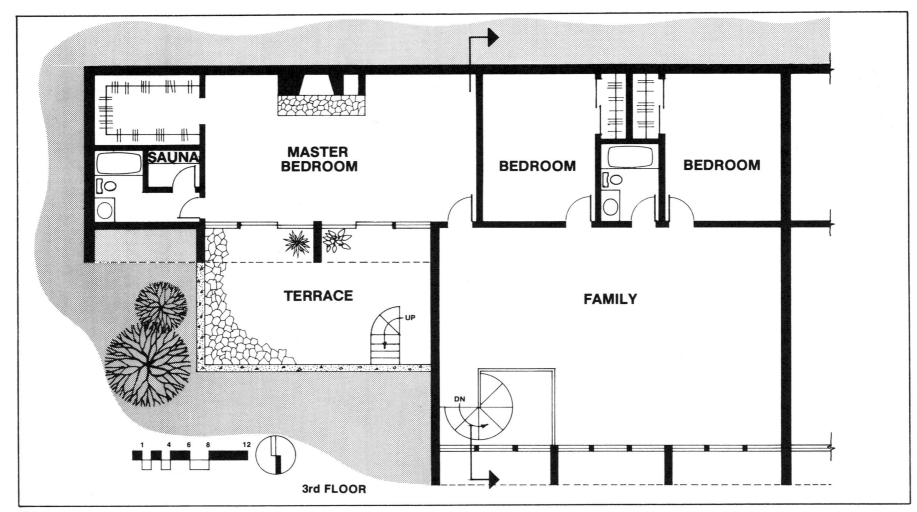

SAUNA

MASTER
BEDROOM

BEDROOM

BEDROOM

TERRACE

UP

FAMILY

DN

1　4　6　8　12

3rd FLOOR

Perspective

Mediterranean Villa

Description

A number of earth shelters have been built utilizing various methods to create a barrel vaulted structure. The Villa represents what can be accomplished using sprayed concrete over metal forms placed in the basic culvert shape. Since the barrel shape is basically strong in compression, the roof area can withstand greater loads. Several vaults are coupled together in this floor plan, giving a tremendous feeling of openness inside. Windows and sliding glass patio doors open from the bedrooms and living room onto a terrace and decks on either end of the structure. Because of the height gained in the barrel ceiling, lofts and other storage areas can be neatly hidden away in any room.

3450 Sq. Ft.
Custom plans only

Floor Plan

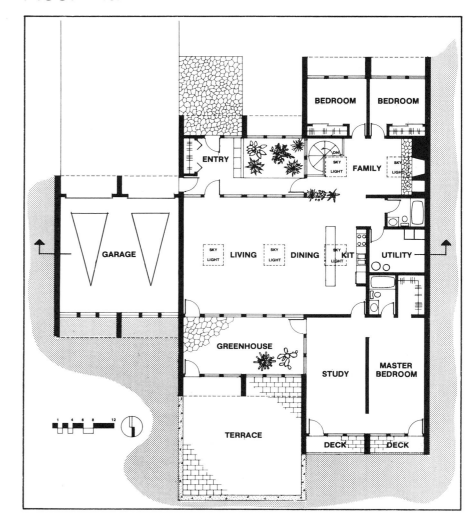

Mediterranean Villa

Section

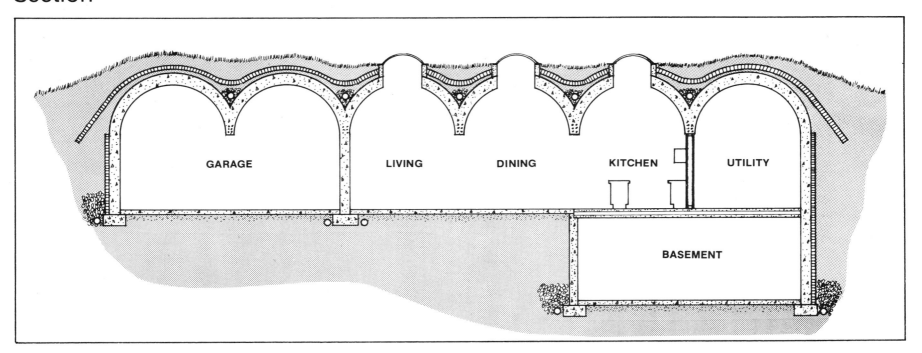

GARAGE

LIVING

DINING

KITCHEN

UTILITY

BASEMENT

Perspective

Ridgecrest

Description

A snug-bright two bedroom economical solar earth sheltered home. This plan is especially oriented to the newlyweds and the retirees looking for a compact relatively maintenance free home. Incorporating a clerestory window arrangement, the rear third of the house and the utilitarian areas are bright and cozy.

1624 Sq. Ft.
Plans available

Section

Floor Plan

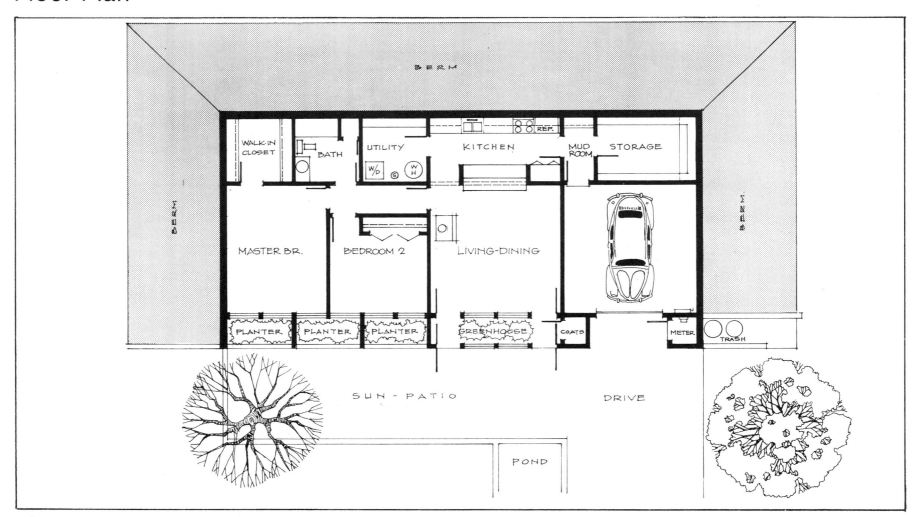

BERM

BERM

BERM

WALK-IN CLOSET

BATH

UTILITY

W/D · S · WH

KITCHEN

REF.

MUD ROOM

STORAGE

MASTER BR.

BEDROOM 2

LIVING-DINING

PLANTER

PLANTER

PLANTER

GREENHOUSE

COATS

METER

TRASH

SUN - PATIO

DRIVE

POND

Monterey

Perspective

Description

A luxurious, two-story clerestoried solar home with three bedrooms; two and a half baths, large two-story living room with conversation pit; balcony, family room and greenhouse. A two car garage, plentiful storage and work space, provides all the amenities conducive to easy living. Terrace on south side and sun trap on north side, make for pleasurable out door relaxation.

**4200 Sq. Ft.
Plans available**

Section

Floor Plan

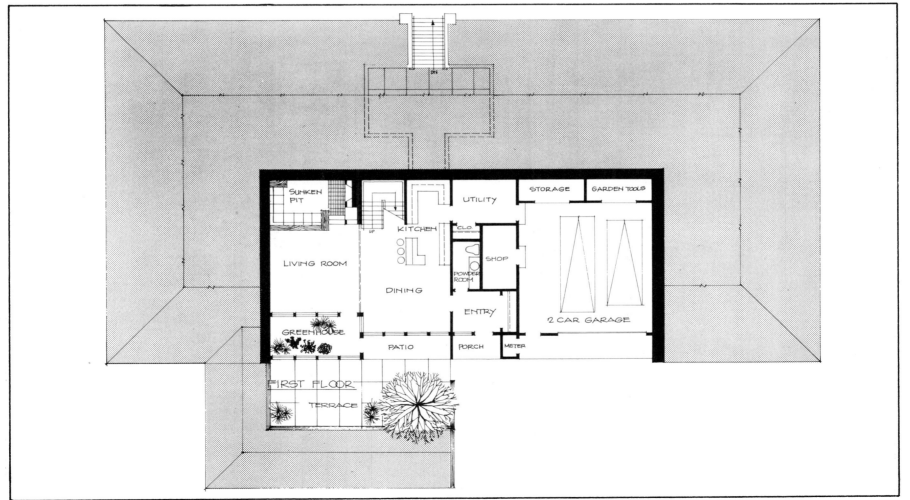

SUNKEN PIT

UTILITY

STORAGE

GARDEN TOOLS

KITCHEN

CLO

LIVING ROOM

SHOP

POWDER ROOM

DINING

ENTRY

2 CAR GARAGE

GREENHOUSE

PATIO

PORCH

METER

FIRST FLOOR

TERRACE

Floor Plan

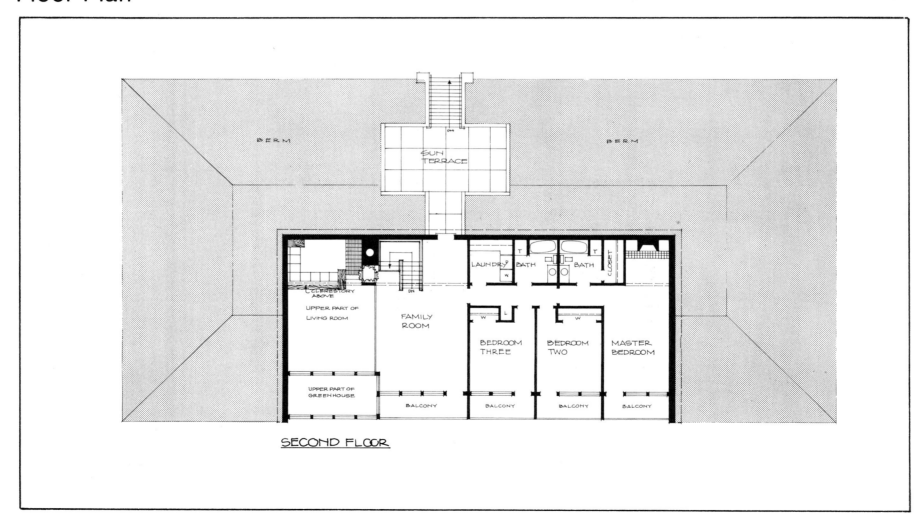

BERM

SUN
TERRACE

BERM

LAUNDRY BATH T T BATH CLOSET

CLERESTORY
ABOVE

UPPER PART OF
LIVING ROOM

FAMILY
ROOM

DN

BEDROOM
THREE

BEDROOM
TWO

MASTER
BEDROOM

UPPER PART OF
GREENHOUSE

BALCONY BALCONY BALCONY BALCONY

SECOND FLOOR

Wood Haven

Perspective

Wood Haven

Description

This three bedroom earth bermed house, with greenhouse and sunken terraces, provides all the space needed for a growing family. Pressure treated wood is used wherever earth touches wood, making this house easy for a novice to build. As shown in Popular Science magazine.

2600 Sq. Ft.
Plans available.

Section

Wood Haven

 38

Floor Plan

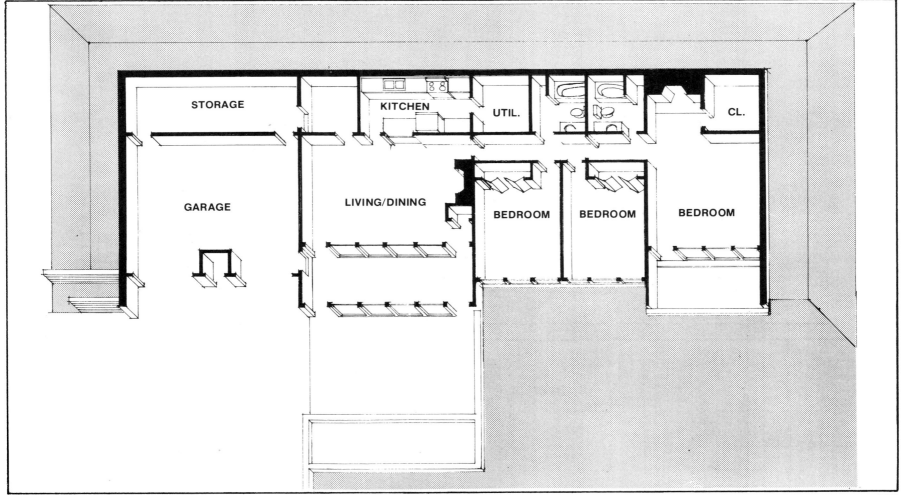

119

Alpine

Perspective

Alpine

Description

A two-storied compact house offering three and four bedrooms, living and dining rooms, and greenouse, designed on four foot modules. It incorporates all the basic amenities for gracious living. As shown in Popular Science magazine.

1920 Sq. Ft.
Plans available

Section

Floor Plan

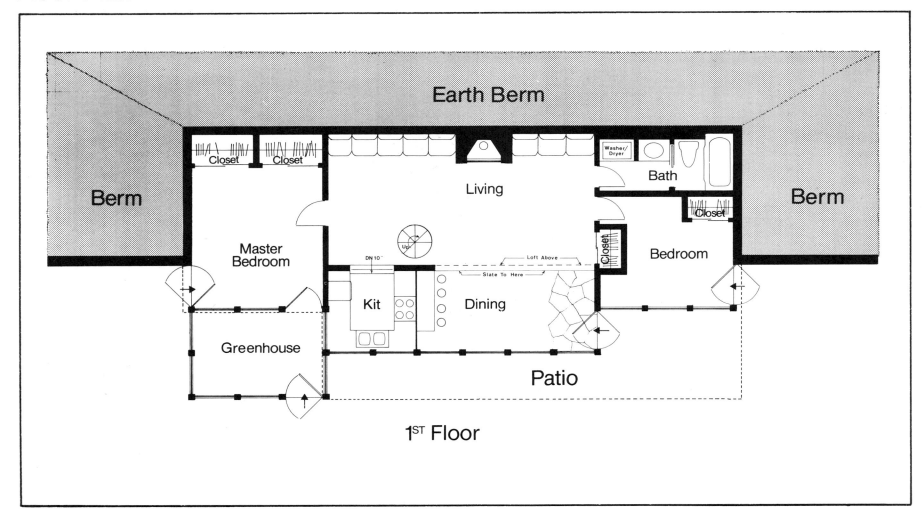

Earth Berm

Berm

Berm

Closet | Closet

Master
Bedroom

Greenhouse

Kit

DN 10"

Up

Living

Dining

Loft Above

Slate To Here

Closet

Washer/
Dryer

Bath

Closet

Bedroom

Patio

1ST Floor

Floor Plan

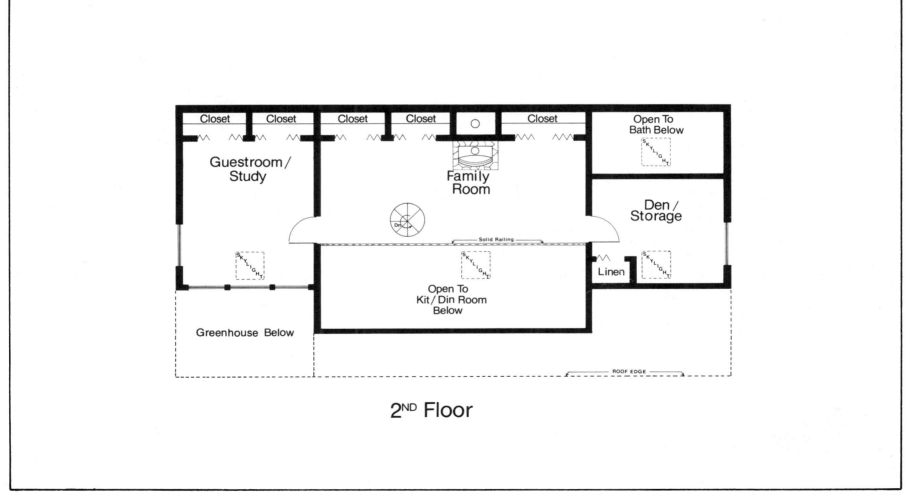

Closet Closet Closet Closet Closet

Open To
Bath Below

Guestroom /
Study

Family
Room

Den /
Storage

Solid Railing

Linen

Open To
Kit / Din Room
Below

Greenhouse Below

ROOF EDGE

2ND Floor

Perspective

Description

This home is a sophisticated but sensibly designed residence. It can be reduced by deleting or delaying construction on the master bedroom portion; or by eliminating the garage and its amenities; or by starting with the basic core of 1350 sq. ft. it can be expanded to meet the needs of the owner. A near zero energy requirement makes this a very affordable house for the economy minded. As shown in Mother Earth News magazine.

1350 Sq. Ft.
Plans available

Section

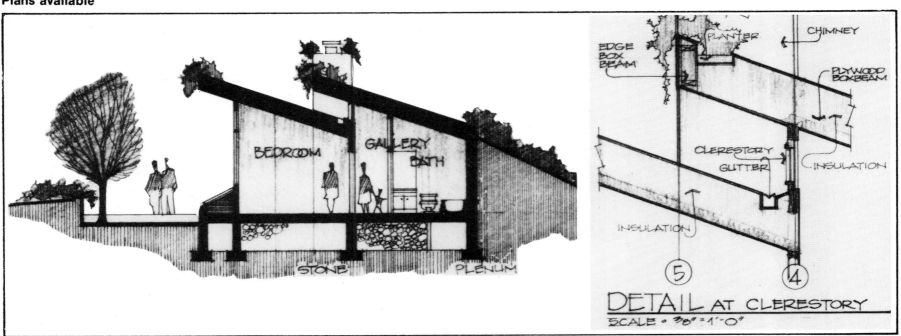

BEDROOM — GALLERY — BATH

STONE — PLENUM

EDGE BOX BEAM — PLANTER — CHIMNEY — PLYWOOD BOX BEAM — CLERESTORY GLITTER — INSULATION — INSULATION

⑤ ④

DETAIL AT CLERESTORY

SCALE: 3/8" = 1'-0"

Floor Plan

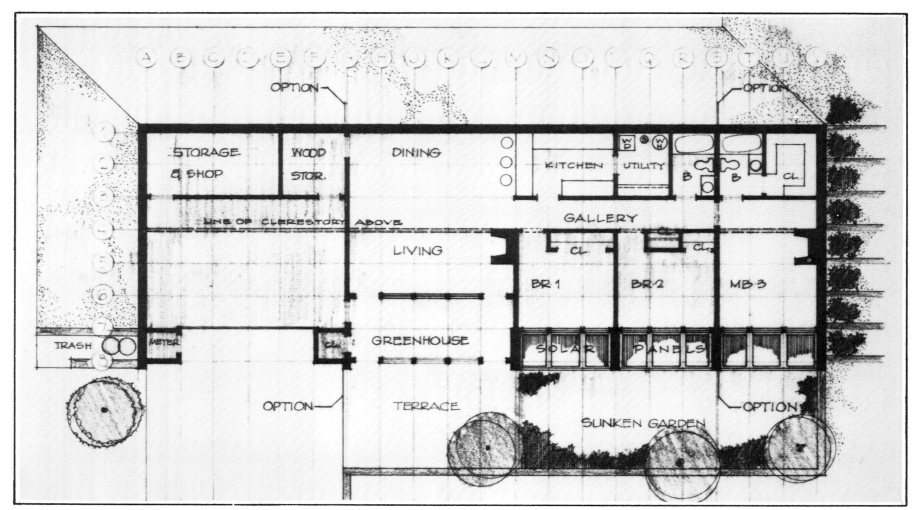

Sample Working Drawings

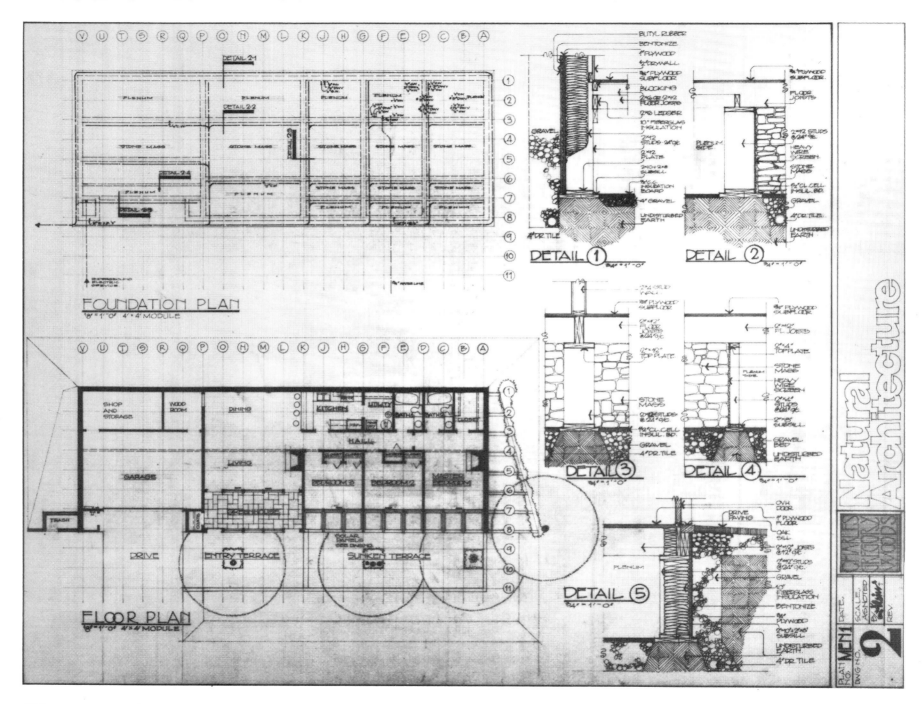

FOUNDATION PLAN
1/8" = 1'-0" 4' x 4' MODULE

FLOOR PLAN
1/8" = 1'-0" 4' x 4' MODULE

DETAIL 1   3/4" = 1'-0"
DETAIL 2   3/4" = 1'-0"
DETAIL 3   3/4" = 1'-0"
DETAIL 4   3/4" = 1'-0"
DETAIL 5   3/4" = 1'-0"

Natural Architecture

OAK'S GREEN WOODS

PLAN NO. MEN1
DWG NO. 2

DATE.
SCALE. AS NOTED
REV.

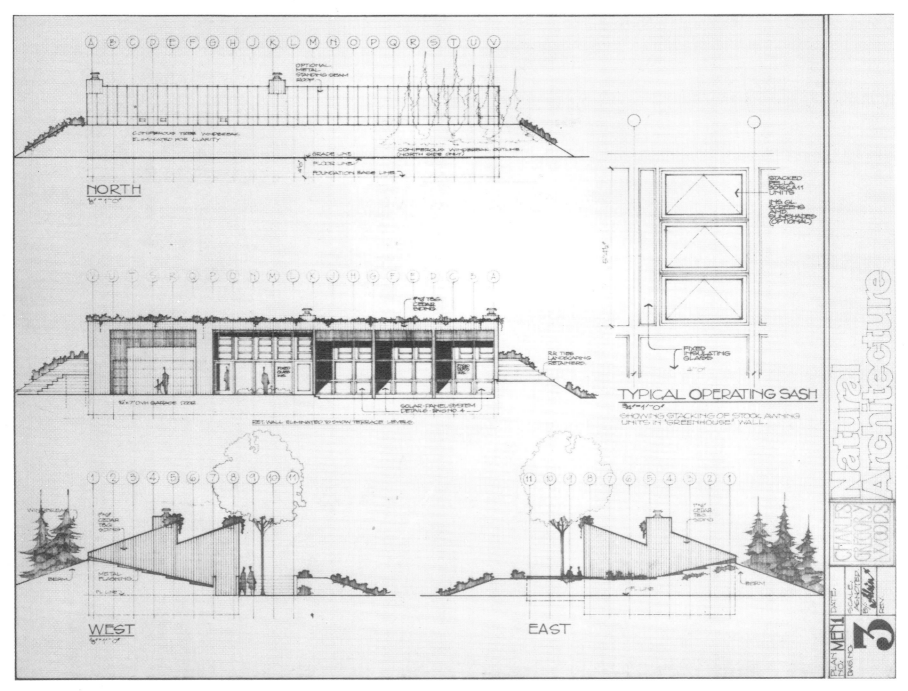

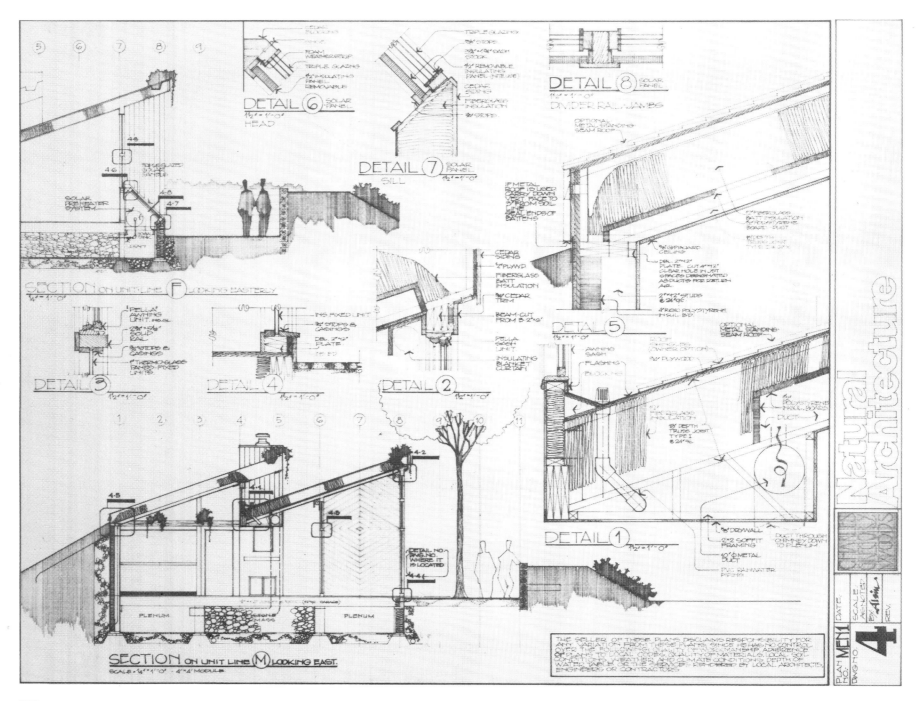

DETAIL 6 SOLAR PANEL
HEAD

DETAIL 7 SOLAR PANEL
SILL

DETAIL 8
DIVIDER RAIL JAMBS

SECTION ON UNIT LINE F LOOKING EASTERLY

DETAIL 3

DETAIL 4

DETAIL 2

DETAIL 5

DETAIL 1

SECTION ON UNIT LINE M LOOKING EAST.
SCALE: 1/4"=1'-0" - 4'x4' MODULE

Natural Architecture

PLAN NO. MEN1
DWG. NO. DWG-10
DATE.
SCALE AS NOTED
ARCHITECT PXAlvin
REV.
4

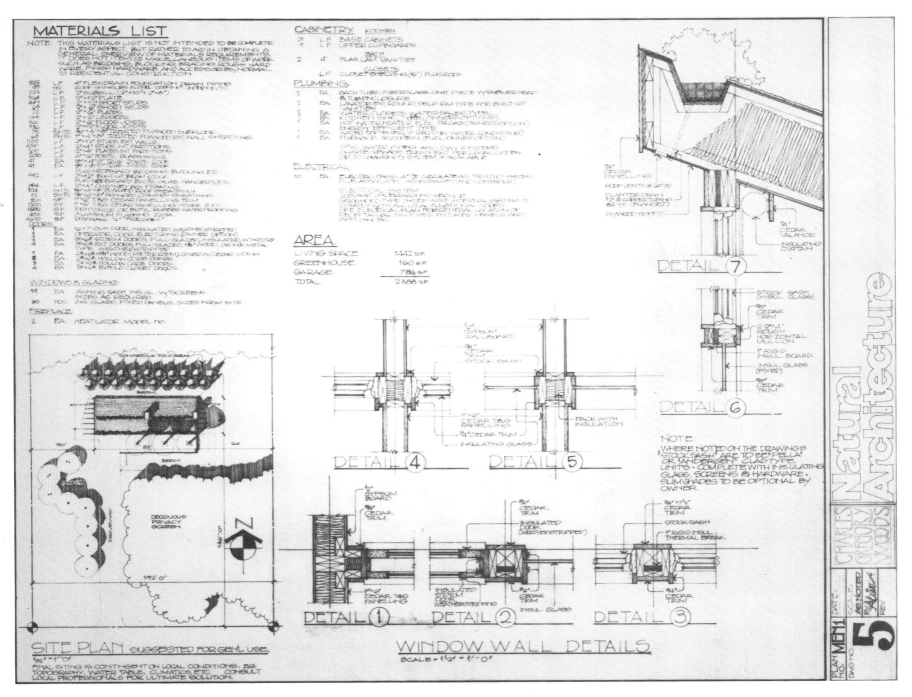

MATERIALS LIST

NOTE: THIS MATERIALS LIST IS NOT INTENDED TO BE COMPLETE IN EVERY ASPECT, BUT RATHER TO AID IN OBTAINING A GENERAL OVERVIEW OF MATERIALS REQUIREMENTS. DOORS, HARDWARE, MISCELLANEOUS ITEMS OF WORK SUCH AS BRIDGING, BLOCKING, SPACING, ROUGH HARDWARE, FINISH HARDWARE, ARE, AS REQUIRED BY NORMAL RESIDENTIAL CONSTRUCTION.

CABINETRY KITCHEN

21	L.F.	BASE CABINETS
11	L.F.	UPPER CUPBOARDS

BATH
| 2 | 4' | PLAS. LAM. VANITIES |

CLOSETS
| | L.F. | CLOSET SHELVING (16") PLUS RODS |

PLUMBING

2	EA.	BATH TUBS, FIBERGLASS ONE PIECE W/SHOWER HEAD & TUBING ENCLOSURE
3	EA.	LAVATORIES, ROUND SELF RIM TYPE FOR BUILT-UP VANITIES
3	EA.	WATER CLOSETS, WATER SAVER TYPE
1	EA.	KITCHEN SINK (PER OWNER OPTIONS)
1	EA.	HOT WATER HEATER, ELEC. OR GAS (OWNERS OPTION)
1	EA.	SHEET, EFFICIENT TYPE
1	EA.	WATER SOFTENER, IF REQD. BY WATER CONDITIONS
1	EA.	FURNACE, 90000 BTU (FUEL, OWNERS OPTION)

CP/C. WATER PIPING AND DWV SYSTEMS
ON-SITE SEWAGE TREATMENT PER LOCAL CODE, OR TO COMMUNITY SYSTEM, IF AVAILABLE

ELECTRICAL

10	EA.	ELECTRIC FANS, ATTIC CIRCULATING THRU DUCT SYSTEM (FLIP ASSY LOCATED, ACCESSORY BATH AND CONTROLS)

ELECTRICAL SYSTEM
200 AMP UNDERGROUND SERVICE
GROUNDED TYPE THREE WIRE INTERNAL SYSTEM TO CONFORM W/LOCAL ELECTRICAL CODE.
SEE FLOOR PLAN FOR GENERAL LOCATION OF RECEPTACLES, SWITCHES, FIXTURES, PANELS, AND APPLIANCES.

AREA.

LIVING SPACE	1442 SF
GREENHOUSE	160 SF
GARAGE	786 SF
TOTAL	2388 SF

WINDOWS & GLAZING

14	EA.	AWNING SASH, INS. GL., W/SCREENS SIZES AS REQUIRED
30	POS	INS. GLASS, FIXED PANELS, SIZES FROM SITE

FIREPLACE

| 2 | EA. | HEATILATOR MODEL NO. |

DETAIL ⑦

DETAIL ⑥

NOTE:
WHERE NOTED ON THE DRAWINGS, STOCK SASH ARE TO BE "PELLA" OR "ANDERSEN" CLAD TYPE UNITS, COMPLETE WITH INSULATING GLASS, SCREENS & HARDWARE. SUN SHADES TO BE OPTIONAL BY OWNER.

DETAIL ④   DETAIL ⑤

DETAIL ①   DETAIL ②   DETAIL ③

SITE PLAN (SUGGESTED FOR GEN'L USE.)

FINAL SITING IS CONTINGENT ON LOCAL CONDITIONS, E.G. TOPOGRAPHY, WATER TABLE, CLIMATICS, ETC. CONSULT LOCAL PROFESSIONALS FOR ULTIMATE SOLUTION.

WINDOW WALL DETAILS
SCALE = 1½" = 1'-0"

CHARLES GREGORY WOODS

Natural Architecture

PLAN MH1 DATE
DWG NO. 5
SCALE AS NOTED
REV.

OUTLINE SPECIFICATIONS

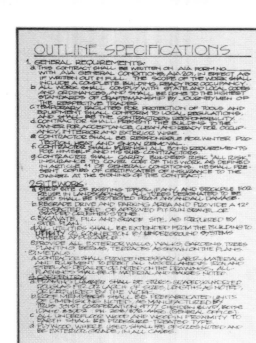

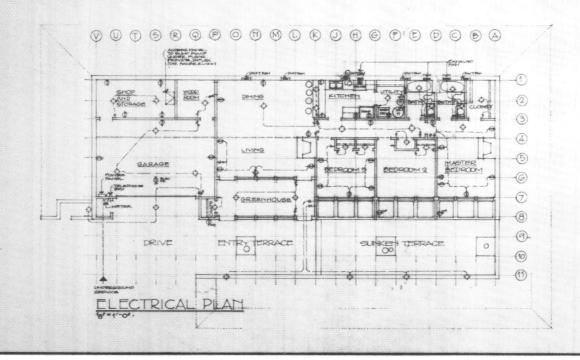

ELECTRICAL PLAN
⅛"=1'-0"

Natural Architecture

CHARLES GREGORY WOODS

PLAN NO. MEN1
DWG. NO. **G**
DATE:
SCALE: AS NOTED
BY:
REV.

132

Suggested Reading

BOOKS

Brooks, H. Allen. *The Prairie School: Frank Lloyd Wright And His Midwest Contemporaries.* University of Toronto, 1972.

Campbell, Stu. *The Underground House Book.* Garden Way, 1980.

Earth Sheltered Housing Design. U/Minnesota. Van Nostrand Reinhold, 1979.

Earth Sheltered Homes: Plans And Designs. U/Minnesota. Van Nostrand Reinhold, 1981.

Earth Shelter Residential Design Manual. U/Minnesota. Van Nostrand Reinhold, 1982.

Gideon, S. Space. *Time And Architecture.* Cambridge: Harvard University Press.

Hitchcock, Henry R. *In The Nature Of Materials: The Buildings of Frank Lloyd Wright.*

The Prairie School Tradition: Sullivan, Adler, Wright and Their Heirs. Editor Brian A. Spencer. Watson-Guptill, 1979.

Rand, Ayn. *The Fountainhead.*

Rudoffsky, Bernard. *Architecture Without Architects.* New York: Doubleday.

Safdie, Moshe. *Form and Purpose.* Houghton Mifflin, 1982.

Soleri, Paolo. *Matter Becoming Spirit.* Anchor Books.

Sullivan, Louis. *Kindergarten Chats, And Other Writings.* Peter Smith.

Twombly, Robert C. *Frank Lloyd Wright: His Life and Architecture.* Wiley & Sons, 1979.

Wade, Alex. *30 Energy Efficient Homes You Can Build.* Rodale Press.

Wells, Malcolm. *Gentle Architecture.* McGraw-Hill.

Wright, Frank Lloyd. *Drawings Of Frank Lloyd Wright.* Horizon.

PERIODICALS

Earth Shelter Living. Published bi-monthly. Subscription: 1 year-$18. 110 So. Greeley, Stillwater, MN 55082.

How To Hire Us

To alleviate a thousand letters and phone calls

Natural Architecture is a design firm headed by Charles G. Woods. We employ an Associating Engineer, James F. Knash, P.E.; Associating Architect Al Sincavage (a competent architect of diversified experience); and our renderings are done by Randolph Padorr-Black (he can draw *anything*); as well as Al Sincavage, Jay Boyle and Dave Eurton. Our drafting is done by Warren Heinly and others.

We are pleased to do small, medium, and large projects, as long as they are earth sheltered (or partially bermed), passive solar or of an energy efficient type. Our work has been shown in magazines, newspapers, and now in this book, *Natural Architecture*. We have offered professional basic working drawings at an economical price ($100-$150) in various magazines -- *Popular Science, Hudson Home Guide,* and *Earth Shelter Living*, to name a few.

For our custom residential, commercial or institutional design services, we work this way:

We charge 10% of the total cost of construction including all accessories and an additional 2% or more for supervision of the project. In addition, we require a minimum of $500 retainer fee (deductible from architectural fee) and charge for reimbursible expense — plane fare, phone, blueprints, etc. This cost is justified by the fact that we can actually save you money on construction by careful planning. Proper design at the outset, can make the home worth more at time of resale.

Example: If someone wants us to design a house in Minnesota, with well and septic (we design well and septic placement) and it costs $100,000, the fee, if supervision is desired, will be $12,000 plus $1,000-$3,000 in expenses for a total fee of $15,000.

Prices are as of 1983. My houses cost approximately $25 sq. ft. for a shell and $35-$55 sq. ft. for a finished house. All structures use 50% or less heating/cooling than conventional houses.

In addition, a site survey, soil tests and written program will be needed from you before we begin. We then will do as many preliminary designs as necessary to please you, with the final rendering completed in color ink to give you a good idea of what you are building.

Plans are based on 30-pound snow loads and assume good bearing and draining soil. Your design may need to be slightly modified by a local architect or engineer to suit your geographical area. The publisher, of course, is not responsible for plans.

Detailed working drawings are next; even a small house has 7-10 sheets of drawings, with some projects running to fifty sheets or more (as in the case of a large project). We then write detailed specifications, calling for brand names, etc. Finally, we get bids, negotiate contracts, and then supervise construction. It's a lot of work; 3-6 months for a small house, 6 months to over a year on a larger one. So plan ahead, and please give us a month's notice if you want us to do a custom project.

Summary: We have economical plans or we can do complete or partial custom projects. If you like one of our designs, you can purchase the stock working drawings and we will modify the designs for our consulting fee of $50 per hour, usually under $1,000 total.

Charles Woods can be invited to lecture for $250 per lecture, plus travel expense.

We look forward to working with you.

Charles G. Woods & Associates
NATURAL ARCHITECTURE

To Order

Plans include: Perspective, plans, elevation, section details and general specifications.

To order: Please indicate name and number of design*.

1 set — $125, outside U.S. — $150, U.S. funds, payable through a U.S. bank. No C.O.D.'s. Additional sets at purchase time — $25. Detached garage plans (where applicable) — $25 ea. Mailing and handling — $15.

Allow three weeks for delivery.

NATURAL ARCHITECTURE
Charles G. Woods & Associates
R.D. 3, Box 538
Honesdale, PA 18431

Office: (717) 253-5452
Res: (717) 253-3921

You are invited to telephone our office if you have any questions.

Plan Name _____ No. _____

Plan Name _____ No. _____

Plan Name _____ No. _____

Name _____

Address _____

City _____ State _____ Zip _____

Exp. Date _____ Signature _____

 **Natural Architecture**

*Several plans may be available at a later date. Please write if interested in those marked custom plans only.